Sevek Finkel

Sevek AND THE HOLOCAUST
THE BOY WHO REFUSED TO DIE

Published by:
Sidney Finkel
367 Tulip Circle
Matteson, Illinois. 60443
708-955-7408
http://holocaustspeaker.com

Copyediting and proofreading by Ken Keller
Text and cover design by WhiteOak Creative
Printed and bound by Thomson-Shore.

Publisher's Cataloging-In-Publication Data
(Prepared by The Donohue Group, Inc.)

Finkel, Sidney.
   Sevek and the Holocaust : the boy who refused to die / Sidney Finkel.

   p. : ill. ; cm.
   ISBN: 0-9763562-0-1

1. Finkel, Sidney—Biography. 2. Holocaust, Jewish (1939-1945)--Personal narra-
tives. 3. Children in the Holocaust—Biography. 4. Jews--Persecutions--Poland--
Czestochowa. 5. Buchenwald (Concentration camp) 6. Jewish ghettos--Poland. 7.
Czestochowa (Concentration camp) I. Title.

D804.196 .F56 2006
940.53/18/092   0976356201

Dedicated to those heroic teachers who teach their students about the Holocaust and its lessons concerning...

• the consequences of hatred and prejudice

• the need for tolerance, compassion, and forgiveness

• the courage to stand up for what is good and right.

Sevek AND THE HOLOCAUST

THE BOY WHO REFUSED TO DIE

SIDNEY FINKEL

ACKNOWLEDGMENTS

I feel that *"Sevek And The Holocaust-The Boy Who Refused to Die"* would not have been possible without my community of close friends:

Larry Freeman helped me overcome my reluctance to write my story by his sincere insistence that I owed it to future generations. He convinced me that writing a book about my Holocaust experiences would be a way of healing the wound inside of me.

When I began to write, it was Larry's encouragement that made me stick to this project. He would read what I had written, and tell me "You are a first-rate writer and story teller". He took time away from his busy schedule to sit with me at Starbucks and discuss my progress.

My deep gratitude goes to my Editor and friend, Susan Kelly. Sue, a recently retired schoolteacher, was at my house six weeks editing the text. Her work transformed the book into a smooth easy read.

My friend Keith McPherson, a well-known book designer, created the cover and produced my book. Keith's artistry added beauty to the book. The creation of *"Sevek And The Holocaust-The Boy Who Refused To Die"* became urgent when Keith read a hate letter I had received and urged me to write my story.

I want to thank my friend Chris Flor for his support and willingness to help me in any way.

I also want to thank Professor Waltzer of Michigan State University. He discovered me as a result of his research into the saving of the kids in Buchenwald. He read the script of my book and made many helpful suggestions. He also made sure that it is historically accurate.

To my children and grandchildren, who are enthusiastic about the book.

Last, but not least, to Jean- my loving wife of forty years who stood by me and comforted me when the memories of the past became unbearable.

TABLE OF CONTENTS

I was looking up when out of the sky, dive-bombers descended and, as they dove, they made a horrendous, frightening whistling sound. They dropped incendiary bombs and everything around me caught fire. Every one was running in different directions not knowing where they could find shelter. Cats, dogs, horses, and cows were on fire, but they were still running. I don't know why, but I was frozen to this spot and could not move or stop looking upward. When the bombers finished their destruction, fighter escort planes flew down so low that I could clearly see the pilot sitting in the cockpit as he was firing his machine guns at the people, who were trying so desperately to escape the slaughter. Still I stood with my eyes towards the sky.

CHAPTER 1

A REMINDER OF THE PAST

It has been almost 50 years since my six-year experience with the Holocaust has ended, and yet here I was driving to Champaign, Illinois, to meet with my daughter, Ruth and to tell her the whole story of my survival during the Holocaust. Ruth, who at the time of my visit to Champaign was pregnant with my grandson, Ike, was insistent that she know the history of my family and my experiences in the Holocaust. I felt I didn't want to have anything to do with this part of my life. I had separated myself from the survivors when I came to America. So, any time anything would come up on television on this subject, I walked out of the room. The same was true of films and books. I especially didn't want to tell my children. I was scared that knowing my story would put a burden on them; leave them with a sense of responsibility that I didn't want them to feel. After all, when I arrived in England in August of 1945, right after my liberation from the Nazis, I was thirteen years old, and we were all told by the psychologist and social workers that we should forget about the past and just go on with our lives. I thought that was good advice. Why talk about it and expose myself to pain?

When I arrived at Ruth's house I was feeling nervous and a little afraid. However as I aged and my children became adults and parents, I was beginning to feel I needed to pass on this history to my family. Ruth was home by herself, her lovely stomach showing the growth of the child she was carrying. This made me feel safe and comfortable. I told Ruth my story. My story had many holes in it. Because I was young at the time, my memory was faint. Ruth listened to my story with great concentration, and when I finished she had this look of awe in her eyes, but was very pleased that I had shared my story with her. It felt good to unburden myself and have it all come out into the light. Now I felt a closer bond between my daughter and myself.

The Holocaust Museum had just opened in1994, and there was a great deal of publicity about it. Ruth talked with her brother, Leon, and we decided as a family to take a trip to Washington D.C, in order to visit the Holocaust Museum. I was very happy to watch with what eagerness Leon, Ruth, and my wife Jean embraced the idea of us all spending a weekend in Washington, D.C. We arrived there on a Friday; our tickets for the Holocaust Museum were for Sunday.

Ruth and her husband, Scott, were already at the Embassy Hotel; Scott and Ruth were familiar with Washington and acted as guides, showing us all the famous sights. I was very moved by the statue of Abraham Lincoln and just stood gazing at his face with admiration. I read excerpts from his speeches and felt grateful that as a fairly new American, Lincoln had saved the unity of this great nation, and had given me this wonderful safe home.

Even though we were all enjoying ourselves, I could feel my anxiety increasing. We all felt apprehensive about our visit to the Museum the next day. This was the real purpose of our trip. Without knowing specifics, I felt that tomorrow would be a day like no other. It scared me, but I felt good that this time I would not go through it myself. I had my wife and children with me. That night I held Jean very close to me.

Sunday morning we all met for breakfast and from there took the subway to the Holocaust Museum. The subway let us out in the heart of Washington, D.C in the midst of a large crowd of people all going in the direction of Raoul Wallenberg Plaza where the Holocaust Memorial Museum was located. I was pleased the street on which the museum was located was named for the Swedish Diplomat Raul Wallenberg, the man who risked his own life many times to save thousands of Hungarian Jews. I was proud too that my wife's heritage was the same as Raul's.

We entered the museum and took the elevator to the top floor. Even though the exhibits were crowded, I noticed that the crowd was silent. I got the feeling that I was entering a place of awe. The beginning exhibit was historical, telling the story of how Hitler came to power. I felt comfortable with that since I already knew this history. I made comments to my family as if I was a guide with no personal feelings.

We were about to enter the next room when I sighted a railroad cattle car. Somewhere from my memory dread and fear overcame me. Instantaneously, I felt like I was back riding in those cattle cars. This was so frightening for me that I could no longer maintain my normal posture. I ran to Jean and buried my head in her shoulder; tears that were impossible for me to shed before now ran down my face. My family, seeing me so emotionally overwrought all gathered around me. We were all hugging each other. The people near us stood silently and watched. They, too, felt our pain. No one made a comment; there were no questions asked. This demonstration of love from my family made me open up. It was like a gush of water, and all my unconscious emotions rushed forward. I felt wonderful because of the caring by my family members, and for the rest of the tour I told everyone in sight about the meaning of the displays to me.

After three hours of touring we were at The Hall of Remembrance. I was so grateful to the architect who had the vision to build what to me is this holy place. The design lets you meditate in complete silence. Diffused sunlight illuminates the hall as it passes through the translucent glass of a high, center skylight. The hall is circular, like a Greek theatre, with seats all around. Higher up on a ledge are hundreds of memorial candles that we all lit in memory of our lost families. Strangely, not a word was spoken among us. We were so full of feelings and emotions that words at this point were not important. I knew that I would be coming back to this place regularly. I considered this to be the resting place of my father and mother, my sisters, Ronia and Frania.

We went to the cafeteria and ordered sandwiches for us to take outdoors. We all needed to be in the light and among the living. After we ate, I could see that we were all struggling with our emotions. I myself felt that the Museum had opened the pain of the loss of my family. We sat in a circle and in turn expressed our feelings about what we had seen.

Ruth wrote the following: "My dad's story became mine too when he visited me in Champaign. By talking to me that day my father gave me a great gift. He gave me his family. I had two new aunts – Ronia and Frania. I had a grandmother named Faiga and a grandfather named Lieb, who was very kind and patient with my father. He would have been a wonderful grandfather. I just know it. Aunt Ronia was a Zionist who could speak several languages. She was the oldest and my father's favorite. Is this where I get my spirit? Aunt Frania chose to die with her mama and didn't take her sister Lola's hand. How that must have shaped Aunt Lola's life I can only guess.

In our visit to the Holocaust Museum, my father brought my family to life through his voice and courage. Together, the museum and my dad provided a clearer vision of my family's lives, hardships and murders. These people were not somebody else's distant relations. We shared the same flesh and blood. And they had been missing or silent for so long. Now they were becoming a part of me. And now I had to mourn them.

Sitting quietly in the Hall of Remembrance, I recognized the "Catch 22" of the situation. If the Shoah had not been, I would not have been. But the Shoah did happen, and my father has given me the gift of knowing himself and his family, and the responsibility – not the burden – of this legacy."

It was a great trip for Jean and me, and for Leon, Ruth, Scott and Joe, too. They bonded with each other and me, and they carried back with them a sense of our family history.

CHAPTER 2

TELLING MY STORY

Shortly after we returned from Washington to our home in Chicago, Leon called and asked me if I would tell my story to a group of students. I was really torn as to whether I should accept the invitation or not. Part of me wanted to, and the other part was terrified. I had done no public speaking at all, and nothing in my life had prepared me for such an experience. What would I say?

I remembered so little. I was eight years old when the war began and big parts of my life during the six years of the Nazi Holocaust were blocked. Who would be interested in hearing the stories of a little boy? Yet I didn't want to disappoint my son. For the next three weeks, I was a nervous wreck. I would write down some points for my talk, and I practiced out loud as I walked. I walked five to six miles three times a week, and as I walked I would talk out loud. Fortunately there were few walkers this early in the day.

On the day of my talk, I drove with my best friend Harvey, to Francis Parker School, located in the Lincoln Park area of Chicago. I was met by the teacher as soon as I arrived at the school; he escorted me to the music room, which was like a little theatre. I paced back and forth till all the students, about fifty ninth graders, settled down.

I was briefly introduced, and then was totally alone facing these young people. As I opened my mouth I was surprised words came out. I felt like something unseen was directing me. My nervousness left me, and as I spoke, I moved back and forth, using hand gestures to make my points. My point was not to tell the history of the war. I was here to tell them a story about a little kid who survived the Holocaust. As I focused on these students I was pleasantly surprised that they were intently listening. How amazing! They were listening like what I had to say was important to them. I never looked at my notes. Words and feelings that I didn't know I had came gushing out. When I finished, there was a lot of applause and then the questions began.

They thought that because I was a survivor I possessed the answers to the world's problem. Questions covered a variety of topics and many showed great insight. There were questions about why I didn't give up, and did I still hate the Nazis. From the very beginning, I was totally honest about myself. I answered truthfully even if the answer would embarrass me. I told the kids about my emotional suffering and shared with them the fact that I had needed support after my trauma. The student's questions were my favorite part of my presentation. I was flattered when a woman asked me to speak for an organization, Facing History And Ourselves. After the presentation Harvey came over and we hugged. "You made the little girls cry." My head was spinning with excitement. "Harvey, "I said, "I can't understand it, but I have a story that these young people want to hear." Thus began a journey into healing through Sevek's story.

CHAPTER 3 | AN IDYLLIC BEGINNING

I, Sevek Finkelstein was born in Lodz, Poland on December 19, 1931. It was not a good year for a Jewish boy to come into the world. Hitler was soon elected Chancellor of Germany, the depression was at its peak, and it was a rough winter in Poland. My father struggled valiantly to house and feed his family. However, by the time I was six years old, economic conditions had improved, and we were again on our way to being prosperous.

My father's name was Lieb Finkelstein. My grandparents had a business making ceramics and bricks. He was ambitious, and before my dad was twenty years old he acquired enough money to buy a small flourmill that was situated on the river in Pzyglow. The largest population was ten miles away, in Piotrkow Trybunalski.

My father married my mother, Faiga Gold, in 1910, who was a member of a large family with six siblings. My mother and he settled down near their flour mill and began a family. My father was successful and purchased a large farm. Four of his children were born on the farm: Ronia in 1912, Isaac in 1914, Lola in 1916 and Adele in 1918. It was a happy time for the family. My brother and sisters often spoke about how great life was on the farm.

They had their own horses and had all kinds of adventures. I was jealous when later on they told me their stories. I felt that I had missed out on something wonderful.

Poland was under the rule of Russia during World War I and the people wanted to overthrow the Russians and establish a Polish Republic. To that end there were a number of groups that carried on the struggle to gain freedom for the Poles. I heard the story that the three Finkelstein brothers were involved in smuggling arms to the underground. The story must have been true because Alex, the youngest brother, had to flee Poland in a hurry because of his involvement with the Polish freedom struggle. He left behind his wife and four children with our family. Alex's wife and four children, two boys and two girls, stayed with us for four years till their father could send for them. They were extremely lucky to get out of Poland, and their family never suffered through the Holocaust. After the war, Alex's daughter, Eva and her husband Sam were very nice to my sister Lola and me. They sponsored our visas to come to this blessed country.

Upon Hitler's coming to power in Germany in 1933, conditions in Poland became increasingly difficult for Jews. Anti-Semitism was widespread, and special laws were enacted that put obstacles in the way of equal opportunities for Jews. In spite of the prejudice and its impacts on Jewish well being, the Jewish community flourished in other ways --culturally, politically, and even economically. This was a vibrant time for the Jewish people in 1930s Poland, but many longed to have their own homeland where there would be no Jewish persecution.

Propaganda against the Jews became the mainstay of Hitler's reign and there were imitators in Poland. I recall my mother sending me to get some threads from a store that had just opened, thinking they would serve a kid. As I came to the counter and was just about to make the purchase, someone in the crowd shouted that I was a Jew and not to serve me. I departed smarting from the remark.

On my eighth birthday my father surprised me with a pair of ice skates. Prior to this gift my friends and I skated on the soles of our shoes. None of my friends had ice skates, so you can imagine my excitement. I could not wait to feel steel touching ice. My anticipation was short lived since my parents forbid me to go the outside ice skating ring. My parents had fears as a Jew I would be singled out and beaten up. This made me angry but I had to accept it. It would be many years before the opportunity to enjoy skating would present itself.

Actually, there had always been separatism in Poland. Though Jews had lived there for 700 years, at best, there was an uneasy truce between the Polish Jews and the Polish Catholics. Anti-Semitism was widespread and severe. The population of Piotrkow where I lived was about 50,000 people; 15,000 were Jewish. The Jewish community had its own culture that was distinct from the Polish Catholic. Piotrkow had every type of Jewish institution--hospitals, education centers, and many cultural groups. The Jews of Piotrkow were divided between many political groups. From orthodox to secular, from socialist to bourgeois, they all fought for their own ideologies and goals. There were a large number of newspapers mostly in the Yiddish language that were read by the majority of Jews. Most Jews in this town were engaged in occupations such as tailoring, shoe making, and transporting goods around the area. These workers were barely able to make a living. There was also a professional and business class that did better economically. The ordinary Jew in Piotrkow toiled six days a week hoping that his meager wages would be enough to provide for the Sabbath meal.

The Jewish community council was well organized and represented all of the factions in town. The council had the power to raise taxes for the community's needs. The most important duty of the committee was to collect money from people to help the many poor who did not have enough to eat. Jewish education was also extremely important and the committee ran elementary schools and eventually a Jewish high school that accepted the brightest of the students. My siblings went to a private Jewish school known as the Gymnasium. This was difficult for my father and he was often behind in paying.

I was born five years after my sister Frania. It was unusual at that time for a woman to wait five years to have another pregnancy. I have often wondered if she was reluctant to have another child. I don't know. My mother traveled to Lodz, which was the second largest city in Poland, to give birth. My dad wanted to make sure that my mom would have the finest medical facilities available to her. I was born on December 19, 1931.

When I reached the designated age of five, I was sent to kindergarten. I loved going to school. I enjoyed playing with the other kids. And every day I was excited by all the new things I was learning. I was so eager that when I came home, I never stopped telling my mother stories. She would smile at me and run her hand through my hair.

About this time, I was allowed to go by myself to the timber yard my dad owned. It was only a few blocks away, and I loved the adventure. First I had to travel through the open market place. The market fascinated me, especially on Friday when the Jewish women would be there to shop for the Shabbat meal. The smell of freshly baked bread made me want to taste some. I would stand around the stall and when the vendor inevitably saw me, he would beckon me to come closer. Then he would say to the waiting customers, "This is Lieb Finkelstein's youngest son," and he would hand me a big piece of fresh bread. At another stall I would get an apple. I would eat both as I was making my way to Dad's timber yard.

At the yard, I would go to the office where my oldest sister Ronia worked on the books. Ronia was an attractive young person and I felt very close to her. She was the only one in the family who had blond hair and blue eyes, and she could play the piano and sing beautifully. I regarded her as my second mother. Besides her good looks, she was very brave, especially when she confronted my father.

My dad was short in stature but his physique was strong and his temper was famous. I remember once when I was at the timber yard, he became furious with my brother Isaac, who was in business with him. No matter what Isaac did, he was often wrong in my father's eyes. At one point, my father sent Isaac on a journey to buy lumber. He got a great price on the goods and had it sent to us by truck. When Dad saw the truck with timber drive into the yard, he got hysterical. Isaac came running out to see what was wrong, and dad let him have it with both barrels. He called him an idiot and a fool for not having the timber delivered by horse and wagon, since the cost would have been lower. Isaac just stood there, his face all red, just taking it from father. I felt so sorry for Isaac, but secretly I enjoyed the scene. I was thinking to myself, "Wait till I grow up. I will do a much better job, and dad will never treat me like that. I am his favorite." And yet I felt a little frightened. What if I got the same treatment when I became older? I once asked Isaac about how dad's treatment of him, and his reply was that dad was an emotional person, but that he knew that behind his back Dad would always praise him. I have concluded that this behavior was part of our Jewish culture. Parents didn't praise their children but felt they would become stronger from criticisms.

My oldest sister Ronia came out of the office and told my dad to stop behaving like a child. Wow, I thought, that took nerve. Dad immediately became calm. She was not afraid of him. He was like putty in her hands. Later, I told Ronia that I was frightened when Dad was shouting like that. She stood up from her chair, put her arms around me and told me not to be afraid. "You know that Dad loves you so much. He just gets frustrated with the business and all the hatred that he has to put up with. It is so difficult for him. Try to understand, Sevek." The message was lost on me but I loved the time and attention that my big sister gave me.

Ronia was happy. She was deeply involved in the Zionist dream of founding Israel. She was a leader in a youth movement called Hanoar that trained young people to be pioneers in Israel. Ronia told me that she and two of her girlfriends were ready to travel to Palestine, (later Israel) and settle down on a kibbutz. She would be a pioneer. But dad was against the idea. She was torn between the two choices and didn't know what she was going to do. I agreed with Dad; I didn't want her to leave Poland. She was the nicest of my three sisters. When I didn't feel good or something was bothering me, she would always take the time to console me. She paid more attention to me than my mother.

On Friday afternoons the timber yard would close early so everyone in the family would have time to prepare for Sabbath. Walking home with Dad we were greeted by neighbors and friends who wished us a good Sabbath. I didn't like going home because I knew that I had to wait in line to take a bath and dress in my best clothes. I would continually grumble, "Why do you have to have so many sisters? They take forever to get dressed and ready." On the other hand, the house smelled delicious with the aroma of baking and cooking. Dad and I had to hurry to make it on time for the Friday evening services at our Synagogue. I loved to be inside our Great Synagogue. It took the community over a hundred years to build. Dad and I took our seats on benches and looking around me I could see my uncle Rolnik with his three sons, and other family members. Dad took his velvet-covered case and his prayer shawl and covered himself. I sat next to him and he put his arm around me. In prayer, he would spread his shawl over me and kiss me on my head. I felt such a wonderful sense of being loved that I felt the presence of God in my life. I could not follow the prayers that were in Hebrew. As of yet I had no Jewish education. In contrast, there were many poor youngsters, who were taught in small parochial schools. My parents frowned upon this. I would learn Hebrew, as a language, as did my siblings. After a short time I became bored and would sneak out to be with my cousins and other boys. We would play games and have fun. We walked back home but it took a long time since Dad stopped often to exchange greetings.

My mother would spend all day preparing for the Shabbat meal. She would set the table with our finest linens, china and crystal. Flowers would create a beautiful aroma along with the baking and the chicken soup simmering on the stove. The smells of the chicken cooking in the oven would permeate the room. Finally we all sat down at the dining room table. My mother would cover her eyes and say the blessing over the Shabbat candles. My father would welcome the Shabbat with the evening Kiddush over the wine and the Motzi over the special baked bread called chala. My mother's voice sounded so soothing and beautiful to me as she welcomed the Sabbath. Dad would be relaxed and calm and act very caring. Everything was so nice, and I would feel content. Sometimes later in the evening things were spoiled for me when my sister, Lola, would criticize me. She would point out that other boys were polite and well behaved, but I behaved like a savage. I was sensitive to her criticisms though I tried to ignore them. Life was good. I thought that being my Dad's favorite bestowed upon me special powers. I was not like others; I could ignore rules and get away with it.

The food was served by our maid, Sonia, who was a young and pretty Polish girl who I would sometimes follow around. She knew how to read and write, and she would read me exciting stories about cowboys and Indians in a country called America. In many of the stories there were little boys that had their own ponies and rifles. This appeared to be adventuresome. I coaxed Dad to buy me a toy rifle so I could pretend that I was that boy. I loved the rifle, but one day I was running and the rifle hit a door and it broke. I cried because this was the end of my cowboy and Indian fantasy.

My sister Frania was sometimes my pal. She was going to elementary school and would soon be entering the Hebrew Gymnasium. She was quite bossy and ordered me around but I didn't mind. She was a beautiful teenager and attracted boys like bees attract honey. She always had friends around her. She seemed to be always happy and full of enthusiasm and would be in conversation with our mother. The two of them were always together giggling and having fun. I was jealous of Frania--I wished that I could get this close to Mom. There seemed to be an invisible division between Frania and me. I was the responsibility of my dad and she of mother. I didn't like that. I needed and wanted to be with mother too. I was always eager to spend time with Frania, since she would be allowed to go to the one movie in town if she took me along. So I occasionally tagged along with her and a few of her girlfriends. Even though I was five years younger than Frania I felt that it was my responsibility to protect her. I was jealous when she flirted with boys. She was my sister, and I didn't want to share her with other older boys.

In the summer, it would get very hot and many families would leave town seeking cooler places. One such place that the people of Piotrkow would flock to was my mother's home village of Pzyglow. It was situated on a fast flowing river and surrounded by forests. It was a wonderful place to get away from city life and relax. We stayed in a big summerhouse close to the river. Mother was happy to be back where she was born. Some of her sisters were staying in other cottages close by so she had plenty to do. Dad would come with Isaac on Friday night and stay till Sunday. It was a happy time for me; I had cousins to play with, and mother made it Frania's responsibility to entertain me.

In Pzyglow after the completion of Shabbat, the weekend social activities would begin. Frania looked lovely all dressed up. As always, several of her girlfriends would call on her and they would go out. I would walk with them, and on the way she would give me a bunch of pennies and tell me to mark our way so we would know how to get back. I thought that this was a great game and took it very seriously. Out of the darkness of the evening, I came to a wondrous place. There were lights strung on a pavilion, and young people were dancing. What an amazing sight -- the music was so cheerful. I stood there and looked in wonder at all the fun the people were having.

I saw Ronia and Isaac dancing with their partners. The man with Ronia I had seen before in our house--his name was Bob Bluestein. Isaac was dancing with my first grade teacher, Miss Rosenberg. I didn't understand how he could be so casual with my teacher who to me was a sacred person. Miss Rosenberg came over to where I was standing and said "Hello, Sevek. Hope you are having a good summer." Isaac was not that nice. In a stern voice he said "Who brought you here?" Spotting Frania he asked her to take me home since it was getting late. Frania was not pleased with our big brother's request, and for a long time she ignored him. After a very enjoyable evening, we started back home. I wanted to find the pennies I had left earlier, but it was too dark to spot them. I then realized that Frania and her friends had fooled me. I heard them laughing, but I was not mad because I liked so much to be with Frania and her friends.

Later, Ronia married Bob and they had their own modern

apartment. I would plead with Ronia to allow me to spend the night in her new home. It was fun and interesting to be there. They had company with friends dropping by constantly. I loved to listen to the heated political debates that took place, even though I understood little. A lot of the talk was about Hitler and Germany, and how they were treating the German Jews. Ronia and her friends were collecting blankets, food and money for the Polish Jews who were expelled by Hitler from Germany. The Polish Government would not allow them to enter Poland, so they were camped outside the border. Life was good for me when I turned eight. I liked going to my little school, and learning to read and write was very exciting. A whole new world opened up for me. I felt so keyed up that on my way to school I would read every sign above the stores. As soon as school would be over I would run to the timber yard and be with Father, Ronia, and Isaac.

Dad had gotten a German shepherd guard dog for the yard. The dog was on a chain but when the yard closed he was let loose. I was looking at the dog longingly wanting to play with him. Isaac noticed and came over to me, saying "This is not a pet dog. He is here because he has been trained to be an attack dog. He could hurt you badly." I named the dog Tom, after my favorite character Tom Sawyer. For the next week I made it my business to feed Tom his meals. I would get closer and closer to him. At the end of the week, he was jumping all over me and licking me. Everyone in the yard came over to look at us play. Dad just shook his head and went on to deal with customers. Tom and I became the best of friends. I loved Tom so much. I had never had a pet before, and even though he was not strictly a family pet, he was my dog. In school I let the whole class know about Tom. In these days it was rare for Jewish families to have a dog as a pet, so they were all very interested. After school I would bring my friends to the Yard and watch me have fun with Tom. That gave me a sense of importance.

One day I accompanied my Dad to a non-Jewish customer's home where he was going to collect money. The couple greeted us warmly. They asked me what my name was, and when I

answered them, the lady asked me if I would like a glass of milk
and cake. She brought the cake and poured the milk, and both
were delicious. My father looked at me smiling. I didn't realize
till later that I had eaten non-kosher food. This did not bother
me much, and, apparently, it did not bother my father either. We
were not very religious although we observed all the holidays and
we kept kosher.

After I finished the milk and cake, we walked home with my
father holding a brown bag stuffed with banknotes. He was in a
good mood and was telling me about the sister I had not known,
Adele. Tears ran down his cheeks, as he described how beautiful
Adele was, and how broken hearted he was when she died. This
was interesting to me since I had never known the details of her
death. It was a family tragedy because she had died at 13 of heart
failure. Walking with my dad in the evening and hearing his
emotional account of Adele made me feel very close to him. He
was confiding things to me that were difficult for him but made
us feel closer.

Other times he would let me come with him to a well-known
restaurant where he would meet business associates. I recall
sitting at large round table with five people. One of the gentle-
men was a Pole of German ancestry; his name was Schultz. He
and dad did business together. It was helpful in business to have
a non-Jew as a partner. I could tell that dad and Mr. Schultz
respected each other. The big moment was when the waiter
brought a tray of Viennese pastries. Everyone was eyeing me to
see which one I would choose. All the pastries were delicious and
I felt very grown up being among adult businessmen.

CHAPTER 4

THE BEGINING OF THE CHANGE FOR SEVEK

When summer came around this year, dad informed us that we would not be going to Pzyglow. Unknown to me, he had bought a sawmill and a flourmill a distance from where we presently lived. The plant was in a place called Pajeczno and we had to travel by train. Isaac was already there since Dad appointed him the manager. Mother, and the others had gone ahead, but I waited for dad to take me on a train. I was so thrilled; this would be a new adventure for me. Janek, who worked for my dad, picked us up in a German-made car owned by my father. This was unusual because at the time few people owned automobiles. Janek drove us to the Piotrkow railway station, and there we waited for the train.

While we were waiting, I was looking in bewilderment at machines that showed all kinds of chocolate bars behind a glass screen. I tried to get dad's attention as he was speaking with someone. When he turned to me I told him that I wanted a chocolate bar. He told me to put some coins into this machine and to pull the lever. I did so and to my surprise out came a candy bar. I didn't understand how this worked. I thought that there had to be a little man inside the display machine. I told this to Father and he laughed out loud.

The train came and I took a seat by the window. It looked to me as if the trees were running with the train. When we arrived at the station, Isaac was there to meet us. He had brought with him a wagon pulled by a horse. I looked at the horse and thought that the animal looked emaciated. We drove along a dirt road with forests on both sides. The landscape was beautiful. When we arrived, it was late afternoon and Isaac drove the horse to our house. Mother came out with Frania running to embrace Dad, and then me. I was so pleased that Frania and mother were here.

The house was warm on the inside but not as nice as I was accustomed to. I was told that I had to share a room with Frania, which was fine with me. Mother had prepared a nice meal for us, eggs and good rye bread. To me all of this was a new adventure.

In the morning as soon as the sun was up, I left the house and went exploring. The land was large, at least several acres. I stood at the entrance and watched as the peasants drove their wagons loaded with sacks of corn stalks to be ground into flour. I would jump on the wagon and, when the driver looked at me, he would tip his hat. His face and hands were wrinkled from hard work, and yet he smiled at me, and I smiled back. When we reached the flour mill, I got off the wagon and thanked the driver.

Inside I liked watching how flour was made and put into sacks. I walked through the place like I owned it. The workers did not take to me, though, to as I thought they should. One time a worker shook an empty sack over my head, pouring the flour all over my hair. I was not afraid of them and I told this man that I would have him fired. He couldn't do this to me! He just laughed and said "Get out of here you little Jew or I will put you in the grinder." I ran home and when Frania and mother saw me all white with flour they started to laugh. Dad had already left for the city so after I was cleaned up, I found Isaac and told him what these workers did to me. He looked at me and said, "Listen, Sevek, I have enough trouble with these Jew-hating workers, and I am not going to start any more trouble on your behalf." I felt humiliated--Dad would not have treated me like that. This was the first time that I had experienced mistreatment because I was a Jew. I didn't like it, but was able to put it aside.

I continued to be adventuresome and often got into mischief. The saw mill was situated next to the flour mill. I also spent time in there exploring and getting into trouble. On one occasion I saw what I thought was a steering wheel that I could pretend to drive. It was lunch time and the men were taking a break from work. As I turned the wheel I could hear the hiss of steam and suddenly the suspended saws came crashing down. When the workers jumped I realized what happened and with lighting speed I ran out of the mill. My mother hid me when the furious foreman came looking for me.

CHAPTER 5

THE BEGINNING OF THE WAR

On September 1st, 1939, the German army invaded Poland. There was no escaping the war now. The Jewish population of Piotrkow was in panic. Friends and relatives dropped in at our apartment to hear the news on the radio, as few people had radios. I watched their faces and observed as the adults were discussing the situation. They were pessimistic about the outcome. No one had much confidence in the Polish Army being able to stop the German onslaught. Being eight years old I was very patriotic and wanted to believe in our armed forces. After all, Isaac had become a soldier in the army. As I looked down from our second floor, I saw a gathering of the nationalistic Polish Party boasting that Poland would be victorious. We were joyful when we heard that England and France had declared war on Germany.

The next day my hopes were shattered as the German planes flew over Piotrkow. They unleashed terror as they methodically dropped hundreds of bombs. We all ran down to the cellar, but we could still hear the tremendous sound of the explosions. For the very first time I had the realization of what terror feels like.

When the all-clear sounded, we went outside on the street and watched huge fires lighting up the skies. We heard that many people had died that day. We were too terrified to remain in Piotrkow. We could see thousands of people getting ready to leave town, and decided to leave our home and go to the village of Sulejow where my father was born. I vividly recall that walk with Mother, Father, and Frania. As we began to walk, I could see that Dad was right, to have us leave on foot. The road was jammed with people, horses, wagons, and a few cars and they weren't making much headway.

I was walking with dad while Frania was walking with Mother. Dad was in a somber mood but talkative. He was telling me about his early life in Sulejow and how he had struggled to get ahead. He had great affection for his mom, and especially for his father, for whom I was named. I felt sad that I had never met my grandparents. Dad was a bit optimistic; he was a young man when World War I was being fought. He recalled that during the previous war, when the German army occupied our town, the German soldiers had behaved in a decent way to the Jewish community. He expressed his feelings that this time it was much different -- then there was no Hitler and little hatred for the Jews. Our Jewish newspapers were full of reports of persecutions in Germany and Austria. The children were thrown out of German schools. Property was confiscated, and Jews had to wear yellow star to separate them from others.

We continued to walk until we were in the village. It was such a pretty place; no wonder Dad loved it so much. Sulejow was very crowded with this enormous influx of people from Piotrkow. Families were walking around exchanging greetings with people they knew. It had the atmosphere of a festive occasion. I met up with some of the boys from my school, and soon we were playing soccer.

I heard the sound of planes overhead and stopped and was looking up when out of the sky dive-bombers descended and as they dove they made a horrendous, frightening whistling sound. They dropped incendiary bombs and everything around me caught fire. Every one was running in different directions not knowing where they could find shelter. Cats, dogs, horses, and cows were on fire, but they were still running. I don't know why, but I was frozen to this spot and could not move or stop looking upwards. When the bombers were finished with their destruction, fighter escort planes flew down so low that I could clearly see the pilot sitting in the cockpit as he was firing his machine guns at the people who were trying so desperately to escape the slaughter. Still I stood with my eyes towards the sky.

I thought I could hear my mother shouting at the top of her voice for me to get down, but I could not move. I felt my mothers arms grasp my shoulders forcing me to get down. I was lying flat on the ground when I felt my mother fall on top of me, covering me with her body to protect me from danger. I hugged the earth and just lay there feeling such fear as I never felt before. My mother's body on top made me feel secure. My mother was also crying softly, and I could feel her tears on me as she was kissing me. I could see from the corner of my eye that my sister Frania was crying hysterically, and Mother stood up and ran to her.

I wanted to stand up and run after her. This was not possible because I was paralyzed with fear. I don't know how long I lay on the ground. I could feel the heat from the fires that were raging near by. I could hear people's voices crying out in pain, but the strongest memory was the smell of burning flesh. When I finally stood up, I was by myself. I felt a powerful anger surge through me. Where was my dad? Where were Frania and my mother? And why did my mother abandon me so cruelly? Didn't she love me? I walked through the village and looked at the corpses. I was so angry that I had no feeling for these poor people.

Suddenly I heard my name being called from a distance. I could see my father running towards me. He hugged me and picked me up in his arms and ran with me into the nearby forest. Dad didn't put me down till we were deep in the forest. There were many of our neighbors in the woods. Dad found a family that he knew and we sat near them. People were telling us that thousands of people had died; whole Jewish families were wiped out. It was a massacre.

I wanted to know where mother and Frania were, but no one knew. Dad saw that blood was coming out from under my hair. Apparently, a piece of shrapnel had hit my head lightly. I was lucky. I recovered in a few hours, but I didn't feel well. My head was hurting, but there was nothing anyone could do for me. We slept on the ground, and in the morning I felt better. I looked around at the hundreds of people near us. I spotted a Polish

Army unit near by and went to look at them. Their faces showed the defeat that they had suffered. I came closer wanting to ask them if they knew Isaac, but one of the soldiers cried out "Get away from here, you damn Jew." My feelings were hurt. I had a brother that was fighting the Germans and yet this soldier could be so cruel. My life was sharply changing and I didn't understand why. I had for the first time felt deep pain, and I didn't like it. I must protect myself and not feel so much, I thought to myself.

There was not much to eat in the forest so I complained to Dad that I was hungry. He took me by my hand, and we walked through the wood to a clearing where we saw a little hut. Dad knocked at the door, and an elderly lady and a man opened it. They looked at us with suspicion, but father smiled at them and assured them that we just wanted to know if they would sell us some food. He took out some bank notes from his pocket and showed them to the lady. She asked us to come in and told us that all she had were some potatoes and sauerkraut. I was not acquainted with this type of food, but since I hadn't had much to eat in two days I was not choosy. We sat down on a bench at a rickety table. The hut was very primitive with a dirt floor, just a few sticks of furniture, and no running water.

When she served us the food, I thought it was the most delicious meal ever. We thanked the couple, and Dad offered some money to them, but strangely they would not take it. We were their guests they insisted. We thanked them profusely as we left. After staying in the forest for three days, we thought it safe to return to Sulejow. We made our way into the village, and there we found a shocking sight. All the buildings were damaged, some completely destroyed. We saw men digging large trenches where the bodies from the bombardment were being buried in a mass grave. We were told that 3000 had perished. I saw men, women, and children who had lost arms, legs, and other parts of their bodies. The worst were the children who were burned. They were in such agony. I looked around at all the destruction and was wondering how could I have escaped it?

☐ Yes, I want _____ copies of *Sevek and the Holocaust: The Boy Who Refused to Die* at $9.95 each plus $2 shipping per book. Orders of 10 or more books are $7.95 per book plus $1.50 shipping per book. Please allow 10 days for delivery.

☐ My check or money order payable to Sidney Finkel for $_____ is enclosed.

Name _____

Organization _____

Address _____

City/State/Zip _____

Email address _____ Phone _____

Please mail this form to Sidney Finkel, 367 Tulip Circle, Matteson, IL 60443.

To schedule Sidney as a speaker, contact him at (708) 955-7408 or S341F@aol.com.

Dad was asking people if anyone had seen his wife and daughter. What had happened to them? Were they among the 3000 people from Piotrkow who had died?

Eventually, we found a person that Dad knew who told us that he had seen Mother and Frania get on a horse-drawn wagon, trying to make their way north to the Russian side of Poland to escape the Germans. I didn't care where they were; they had deserted father and me, and I would no longer think about them. Strangely, I was already forgetting them. I would function in a man's world only. I would miss the feminine warmth and love of a mother and a sister, but in time I would get used to it, I thought.

We were able to get a ride back to Piotrkow on a horse drawn wagon. The man sensed how unhappy I was and allowed me to sit up front and handed me the reigns. When we came to our building, we were shocked to see that only half of it was still standing. The other half was totally bombed out. Seeing our apartment and our belongings gone was too much for Father. He stood looking at the wreck, openly crying. He asked a neighbor to take me to my Aunt Rachel's house. He would stay behind and see if we could salvage anything from the apartment.

On seeing me, my aunt took me into her ample arms hugging and kissing me. It felt so safe to be in my favorite aunt's house. I went inside and the first thing my aunt did was to strip off all my clothes and thoroughly wash me. I hadn't washed for four days. It felt good to be clean. My uncle Israel Rolnik and my cousins, Shlomo and Israel, sat down at the kitchen table, and my aunt served us delicious potato soup, black bread with butter and milk. They all listened as I told them about all that had happened to us. They asked me about my mother and Frania. My voice hesitated and I felt like crying, but didn't, and told them what I knew. My uncle told me that the Germans had arrived a few days ago and that they immediately set fire to the Jewish quarter, and shot the people who were trying to escape. They were going into homes and helping themselves to whatever they wanted. They were terrorizing the Jewish population, especially the religious ones. Aunt Rachel told her husband to stop frightening me, but how could I be frightened after all I had experienced? Aunty put me to bed and covered me with a soft blanket. I could not sleep that night. The mattress was too soft. I had quickly become used to sleeping on the forest floor. I took my pillow and blanket and made myself comfortable on the floor. Dad had sent a message to tell me that he was spending the night in Ronia's apartment. I tossed and turned, but sleep would not come to me.

From now on nothing would be the same for me, my family and the community. I could never have imagined what lay ahead.

CHAPTER 6 | THE GHETTO

The Nazi administrator announced that Jews in Piotrkow could live only in a designated area known as the Ghetto. Most of the Polish people who resided in the Ghetto were removed. Where 5000 Poles lived, now 20,000 Jewish people had to reside. The ghetto contained 182 houses and 4178 rooms, nearly five people per room. We were lucky to have three rooms in a house that used to be my school. We had a kitchen and a bedroom where the whole family slept, and a little porch looking out to a square. Our living quarters had no running water or toilet. It was my job to go outside to the well where there was a bucket with a rope attached. I would lower the bucket into the well and scoop up water.

There were quite a number of kids living in the square, and I would play with them. As months went by, the Nazi authorities would come with new edicts affecting our lives. My dad's property was taken away from him; all we had left were personal belongings and some money and valuables that we were able to hide. I think that Dad had anticipated something like this when he sold his timber yard to Mr. Schultz.

My mother and Frania came back to us, but I don't recall exactly when. It seems that I was still very angry at them for leaving me. I remember my mother sewing a yellow patch on my jacket with the letter J for Jew on it. I didn't know what it was. At first I thought that it might be a badge of honor, but then, later I learned that it identified me as a Jew.

Despite what was happening I have some warm memories of my families' life. Many of the Jewish traditions that were a large part of our lives continued. In the Jewish religion, Friday at dusk

and all day Saturday the Sabbath is observed. Of great importance is the Shabbat meal. At dusk on Friday all activities were
halted in honor of the coming of Shabbat. I was given a small
part in the preparation of the meal. My mother would take a
large pot and fill it with potatoes, chicken, beans, and whatever
fat pieces were left over. After it was covered by brown paper I
would carry it to the bakery. The brick ovens were shut down,
but remained warm from previous baking. The pot would be
placed in the oven and allowed to simmer over night. Saturday
morning after services, the Jewish community would make their
way to the bakery to retrieve the pots. I carefully carried our pot
with delicious aromas filling the air. At home I would wait impa-
tiently till the meal was served.

There would be no further education for me or for other
children in the Ghetto. For the next six years there would be no
schooling. I could read and write a little Polish, but that was it.
In spite of the danger some brave teachers set up some illegal
schools and continued to teach.

Life in the Ghetto over time became much more difficult.
We were only allowed to leave the Ghetto for two hours, and
we had to be off the streets by five in the afternoon. When five
o'clock came, the streets were deserted. I could see people
rushing to be in their homes when five o'clock struck. Signs
were posted everywhere prohibiting Jews from normal activities such as walking on sidewalks. Jews that were caught after
that hour were shot. It seems like there was one punishment--
death.

We often believed that things could not get worse, but we
were wrong. Because of overcrowding, and the lack of soap and
hot water, diseases such as typhus and tuberculosis became widespread in 1941. At that time I was close to a girl, named Hannah.
She and I became constant companions. She was pretty and had
long pigtails that I sometimes pulled on. I used to steal food from
our house and bring it to her. One day I didn't see her and I
become very concerned. I saw a sign on the door that said that
this dwelling was quarantined. I understood that meant that the

people inside had typhus. A few days later the burial people came to her house and carried her away under their arms. I felt such a loss; I would never see Hannah again.

The Nazi authorities established a Jewish Council of prominent citizens who administered the Ghetto. The council was very important in our lives. It allocated food and housing and regulated our lives. The Council received its orders from the Nazis and used bribes to make our lives more tolerable.

Before the closure of the Ghetto I would walk over to the Polish side and spend hours walking on the pavement and looking for cigarette butts. I would collect them in my pocket and bring them home. I would extract the little tobacco that it contained, and when I gathered enough I would make cigarettes. I would stand on the corner of a busy street with other boys and sell the cigarettes for cash. This allowed me to feel a sense of importance.

Eventually the Ghetto had been completely closed, and we were not allowed to leave without special permission. Jews caught outside the Ghetto were shot. Since there was no way to make a living, people got by selling the few things that they had saved. That was also true for my family, but we were better off than most because dad's friends like Mr. Schultz, now a German citizen, would bring us food, and give us money. He didn't have to do so, but he was an honorable man. The biggest industry in the Ghetto was smuggling. The smugglers took a terrible risk because if they were found outside the Ghetto, they faced certain death. And yet things were so desperate and the profits from smuggling were so great, many took the risk.

My parents lost money after being engaged with a smuggler. They responded to this loss with screams of lamentation that frightened me. This experience had a powerful influence on me. For the first time I came to believe that money was of great importance to survival.

My oldest sister Ronia who was married lived with her husband in separate lodgings. I saw her often, and she remained the same loving sister that she was before the war. The family got the news from Ronia that she was pregnant. Under normal circumstances this would have been a very joyous occasion. My parents' first grandchild! However, the family was afraid because being pregnant or the appearance was against the law. This was not a time to bring a child into the world. Ronia nevertheless was happy to be pregnant. Our friend, Mrs. Novak, who was a Pole made arrangements for Ronia to be admitted to a Catholic hospital outside the Ghetto where we felt she would be safe. This was a very courageous thing to do. Poles that helped Jews, if caught, could be killed. It was easy for Ronia to pass as a Pole. She had beautiful blue eyes and blond hair. Ronia was smuggled out of the Ghetto and admitted to the hospital. She gave birth to a boy, and at ten years of age I was an uncle. Tragedy struck when someone in the hospital informed the Gestapo (Nazi security police) that there was a Jew there pretending to be a Pole. The Gestapo came to the ward and picked up the infant who was only a few days old. They threw him out of the window. They then took Ronia to the Jewish cemetery and they shot her.

For months no one would tell me what happened to Ronia. They felt that lying to me was better. Eventually I found out the details. My first reaction was fury. Ronia was gone from my life forever. I dropped to the floor and cried for a long time. My mother and father tried to comfort me. They were crying too, but I didn't want them close to me. I wanted to be left alone. This was to be the last time that I could feel enough to cry.

The longer we lived in the Ghetto, the more independent I became of my parents. I was doing things without first consulting with Dad. I had become good friends with Harry who was my age. I liked his gentle manners and good nature. Harry told me one day that a glass factory outside the Ghetto was recruiting youngsters who were good runners. We were both ten years old at the time, but Harry was bigger. We both decided that we would volunteer for this work and see what it was like. We lined up with a group of older kids. Soon we were marched out of the Ghetto to go work at the Hortensia Glass Works.

My first view of Hortensia was of a huge busy place with workers rushing around. In the middle of the factory was a huge circular furnace. The glass blowers would use a long iron rod to collect the material and blow it into glass. At this point the material was put into a mold, which was an extremely hot liquid and later would form into the shape of a glass. Since the Polish workers were paid by the piece, they were not happy when a glass was lost. It was my job to pick up this hot glass on a fork and run to the conveyer belt. If I was not quick enough the glass would shatter. When that happened I would sometimes be struck over the head.

Another experience in the Ghetto involved unloading trucks. I worked with a group of boys that were older than I. A much bigger kid was handing down the sacks from the trucks. I took my place in line and when my turn came to be given a sack, he looked at my size and shook his head "Hey kid you think that you can manage this?" he asked. Also the Nazi officer, who was supervising, was looking at me in a disapproving way. The first sack was put gently on my back and I knew that I could manage it. We were as strong as the big kids. The next time I came for another sack, I was boastful about it. The big kid on the truck got upset with my cockiness. He took the sack and threw it at me. The sack hit me in the back, hurting me. I could not hold on to it, and dropped it on the ground. I was furious. I wanted to climb on the truck and beat him up. Apparently, he didn't know who my father was. I was just about to do it when the Nazi officer picked me up by my shoulders and slapped my face. Then he told me to stay in the middle of the square by a well. He took out his revolver from his holster, stretched out his arm and was about to pull the trigger. I stood there waiting for it to happen. I was thinking that I was 9 years old, but my life would now end.

I was given a reprieve when the president of the Jewish Council, Mr. Warszawski happened by. He spoke to the Nazi in a very quiet, confidential way. The Nazi lowered his arm and put his gun back into the holster. I ran home without looking back. It didn't take long for my father to hear the story. He was very angry with me, and for the first time ever, he gave me a thorough spanking. I cried and stayed under the table and refused to come out for hours.

CHAPTER 7

ISAAC'S EXPERIENCES

My family was delighted and relieved by a letter that came from my brother Isaac, while he was recuperating from wounds in a German hospital. He was treated well by the Germans despite all the other atrocities. A year later, after being released from the hospital, he traveled by train to Piotrkow. He had the luck to meet someone who knew where we lived in the Ghetto, and he took him there. His arrival at our home was a huge pleasant surprise to us. Imagine the family's elation that he was standing among us and looking well. My mother and father were very emotional, crying with tears of joy.

Isaac still had his Polish uniform on except that he, too, was wearing a yellow badge that identified him as a Jew. We all crowded around Isaac hugging him and making him welcome. Mother was able to make a very nice dinner in his honor. After dinner Isaac lit a cigarette and began to tell us a fantastic story of survival.

THIS IS ISAAC'S STORY:

Two weeks before the start of the war, Isaac was mobilized and joined the 25th Polish Infantry Division. He was sent the same day to Czestochowa, which is close to the Polish/German border. His unit was ordered to dig trenches and fortifications. At daybreak the German army opened up fire with machine guns. The Polish soldiers had very little equipment to fight back. The whole Division had only two machine guns, and not all soldiers even had rifles. They were ordered to retreat into the woods At this point, the unit was scattered. Many soldiers ran away and went home.

On the fourth day of the war Isaac and a few other soldiers went into trenches together with men, women, and children from the village. The German gunfire ignited the straw that was covering the trenches; the people were desperately struggling to escape. As they emerged the Germans machine guns fired and killed all the civilians.

Isaac threw away his rifle and had his hands up signaling that he was surrendering. But it made no difference to the Germans who shot him three times in his right leg. Isaac was also badly burned on his face. He dropped to the ground thinking that he was dead. He lay perfectly still, not breathing when the Germans came around and kicked him several times with their boots, and then they removed his ammunition belt. They left him for dead on the field.

Since it was harvest time, there were stacks of straw stored in the fields. When night fell, Isaac slowly dragged himself and covered himself with the straw. He, thankfully, fell asleep. When morning came, he discovered his hands were swollen and burned, and his trousers were full of blood. He believed there was no chance of survival. He crawled to a road where he saw German soldiers moving. He had no choice but to surrender to the Germans, otherwise death was certain. The German soldiers ran up to him with their guns pointed. He spoke to them in German. He cleverly lied and told them that he was a Pole of German origin. They believed him since he spoke German well. They picked him up and placed him in a military vehicle and drove about twenty miles where there was a Polish pharmacist. The pharmacist looked at him; he didn't think that Isaac would live. He called a Catholic priest who wanted to give him his last rites. He confided in the priest, that he had lived his whole life as a Jew and would prefer to die as one. The priest understood and blessed him.

A few hours later a German ambulance transported Isaac to a German Hospital. Isaac was immediately taken to surgery. The surgeon asked him his name, and continued with the surgery, despite knowing he was a Jew. The German nuns that ran the hospital treated him kindly. In contrast the Nazi nurses would not go near the Jewish prisoners. Isaac was also able to have conversations with wounded German soldiers, but only when he spoke to them individually.

Isaac told us when he was discharged from the hospital he heard that just two days before, Jewish prisoners of war were let go from a prison camp, made to put on civilian clothes, and were all shot.

I felt more secure with my brother's return to the Ghetto. After all he fought in a war and survived. His friends from school were in the Jewish Police force and made life easier. Because he was a wounded prisoner of war, he had permission to leave the Ghetto and seek aid from the Red Cross for his wounds. He met with non-Jewish friends he had known previously. Later these connections would help in our survival. Isaac had meetings with Mr. Schultz, who by now was a German citizen. We received money from him because of Dad's previous business dealings. This was a kind act because under the present conditions, he was not obligated.

When 1942 arrived, we had lived in the Ghetto for more than three years. As strange as it might seem, we had adjusted to the harsh conditions of life. The Ghetto was becoming extremely crowded with new refugees from other towns and villages. The council did all it could to accommodate these newcomers, but the congestion was impossible. Many had to live in doorways of buildings and outside. There were thousands of them. We all tried hard to help these unfortunate people by taking a few into our own very crowded space.

The Jewish will to survive is incredible. We had been put to the test for so many centuries. In spite of the suffering, especially by the new arrivals, there were a number of people that did well. The best tailors, shoemakers and other tradesmen were in demand because of the German officers desire for luxury goods. Life for these people was good, despite the fact that others were starving.

In the late spring of 1941, German military forces suddenly attacked an ally, the Soviet Union. I watched for hours as an entire division of the German army moved through our street. There were many horses that pulled wagons; I had never before seen such huge and powerful horses. Huge numbers of artillery and hundreds of trucks with troops went by. I was one of a few that watched this German movement. Though most people stayed indoors I couldn't resist the march. An officer riding on a horse shouted for me to get off the street. I was amazed that there could be such a huge army in the world. How I wished that they were Polish.

With the invasion of Russia, the whole attitude of the Nazis changed for the worse. Before, there was a slight tolerance towards the Jews, but now they acted with even more cruelty than before. Beatings and shootings were common. My cousin Nathan, the oldest son of my Aunt Rachel, was caught outside the Ghetto and shot.

My dad's friends used to meet with him in our kitchen to discuss all the rumors that were heard in the Ghetto. While the men were talking, the lights went out. When the light came on, a man at the table remarked our liberation will feel like we had gone from darkness into the light. His words made a deep impression on me.

We watched with fear during 1942 as other Jewish ghettos were being liquidated. The whole Jewish populations of these towns were loaded into boxcars and sent further north. The Nazi authority in Piotrkow told the Jewish council that these trains were going to new labor camps out east. We were told that our turn to be evacuated would come soon. The Germans said they would consider leaving behind about 1500 Jews who would work for the German war effort in factories.

The panic now spread. There were stories that these trains were not going to any work camp, but the people were all killed. Every day there were rumors of instances of people escaping from this death camp, called Treblinka. Most of us refused to believe these extreme accounts. We were taught to believe that the Germans were civilized people. . They would not kill a large population of men, women, and children. We told ourselves that it made no sense to murder people that could be slaves for the German war efforts. And yet we could not totally deny the evidence that became stronger each day that these rumors were likely true. Young women were dying their hair blond in order to appear more Christian when they escaped to the outside. People were obtaining false Christian birth certificates and going to great length to avoid being put on the trains. The Jewish council succeeded in increasing the amount of work permits to 2000. Out of 20,000 people in the Ghetto, maybe 2000 would find refuge.

I know that my family at this time consisted of Father, Mother, Lola, Isaac, and Frania. I also know that Isaac was very busy trying to find a place that would give us work and a precious work permit. Towards that end Isaac was able to contact the Kapatloski family which owned a wooden barrel factory not far from the Ghetto. The Kapatloskis made big wooden barrels for storing beer and other products for the Germans. Isaac was acquainted with the four sons who agreed to go to the German authority and obtain their permission to have Jewish workers for their factory. He was successful in obtaining twenty work permits, but instead of handing them out, the owner demanded money from Isaac for them. Isaac felt that it was insulting for him to ask for money when their labor would be free. However, these were not normal times, and a work certificate could save one's life. So Isaac and Dad obtained two work certificates; I did not receive one, as I was only 11 at this time. Work permits were issued only to those who were thirteen years of age or older. Like an hourglass that was running out of sand, our time in Piotrkow was getting shorter. The death cars were moving closer to us.

The Holy Jewish holiday of Yom Kippur was upon us. In our religion this is the holiest of days. On this day, we fast and spend the whole day in the synagogue, praying to God to forgive our sins. Our beautiful main synagogue was turned into a horse stable by the Nazis, but there were little houses of prayer that we went to. Our whole family was attending these solemn services. The men covered themselves in prayer shawls and prayed, imploring God to forgive us our sins; people unashamedly cried out loud. I was sitting on the left side of Dad, Isaac on the right. Dad and Isaac were rocking back and forth as they prayed. Tears were running down Father's face as he beseeched God to save us. The whole congregation was in tears, some beating their chest with their hands imploring God for a miracle.

I was eleven years old and could not follow the prayers as I didn't know any Hebrew. If things had been normal I would have attended Hebrew school to learn about my religion. Dad made me repeat some Hebrew words, and it felt good to utter these holy sayings. I prayed with my own words talking to God. "Dear God I might not be very deserving like others, but I always loved YOU. Please save our family and the community. We have suffered so much already, isn't it enough?" Listening to the anguish of these people, I thought that God would hear us and respond. When we left the prayer house and returned to our home to end the fast, Lola, Frania, and mother met us.

| # DEPORTATION

Our prayers were not answered. Tuesday Oct 14, 1942, is a date that will live forever in my memory and that of the Jews of Piotrkow. Early the next day the Nazis took up positions around the Ghetto. Even before the deportation they amused themselves by firing indiscriminately at any target. We were confronted by a highly trained group of murderers. First Jewish policemen passed through the Ghetto and ordered the residents to present themselves at the deportation square next to the Jewish hospital. People went to great length to avoid the roundup. Some hid in buildings and others checked in to the hospital and underwent surgery, hoping this would be their salvation. These Jews were not spared either. They were taken and shot on the spot.

We said our last goodbyes; we were all in tears. We now became certain that our fate was sealed. Mother had been preparing food that she put in a rucksack for our journey. Mother talked to me and said, "You must be brave, Sevek, and not make a fuss. You are young and I want you to promise me that you will not do anything foolish. You will do everything you can to survive. You are our future." I wanted to go with my mother no matter what, but it had been decided that I would stay with Father and Isaac. I had no choice; all decisions were made for me regardless what I wanted. Dad and Isaac had their precious work permits that were issued by the Nazi authorities, and they hoped that they could take me with them to their work. Yet my heart was breaking with longing to be with my mother and sister.

When we had to separate from each other, Frania ran up to me and embraced me, kissing my face. "I always loved you and we will all meet again soon." And with these words we parted with the women in our lives. This was the last time I would ever see my mother or Frania again.

There were almost 20,000 people walking to the square on that day in October. Women with children in their arms and husbands who had jobs would be called on to make the most difficult choice of their lives. The men were asking themselves, "What should I do? Shall I go with my family on the train, or should I save myself?" Most families were broken up. Children were torn away from their mothers, wives from their husbands. The SS silenced the cries and screams of the children with kicks from their boots or blows from their whips. Father and Isaac had made the difficult choice to separate from mother, Lola and Frania. The guilt of this decision would stay with me for the rest of my life. In spite of years of counseling I can not let go of this guilt. I have experienced periods of great sadness.

The Nazis with their vicious dogs maintained control. People were being forced and beaten into lines. Men, women and children were organized into separate lines. Under the circumstances no one knew the fate of any line. How could I be saved when I did not have legal permission to stay behind and avoid the death train? How could I be saved when I did not understand the lines?

I was standing with Dad and Isaac in a line, when I was told to stand behind the two. They stood close together and their bodies covered me. I held on to Father's back, shaking with fear. Every few minutes, I would hear a shot and a body fall to the ground. It was a bloody sight with brains scattered everywhere. The screams of the women and children were piercing. I covered my ears with my hands so I would not hear. After a long while a Nazi wearing high riding boots and a leather jacket with leather gloves holding a whip in his hand approached us. Dad and Isaac immediately took off their caps and showed their working permits. He consulted his list and gave instructions to leave the square and go to our working place. Father and Isaac didn't move immediately and as he looked back, he got a glance at me. He came back and using his whip, beating me over the head and ordering me to go to another line. Isaac stepped forward and implored the Nazi to show mercy. "He is my little brother, he is just eleven." And then Isaac took something out of his pocket and put it in the palm of this Nazi's hand. He smiled and ordered us to go to work. We were saved for the present. We would live a little longer. Were we the lucky ones?

Years later I was given the story by my sister Lola how she survived that dreadful day:

My mother Faiga was 46, Lola who was 22 and Frania 16-- were standing together and the police assigned them to the line that was going on the trains. Lola said that she worked as a house-maid and baby-sitter to a high Nazi official. While waiting to be deported, she spotted the man and tried to get his attention. He recognized Lola and came to her. Speaking German, Lola pleaded with this official to save them. He agreed that he would save the two young women but not mother. He said that she was too old.

Lola said that she didn't know what to do because Frania would not leave without her mother. The Nazi official was impatient for them to make a decision. Mother came forward and shouted at Frania to go with her sister. "I can do better without you to worry about," Mother said pushing Frania away. Frania was sobbing and went reluctantly with Lola following the Nazi who placed them in a safe place so they would not be put on the train.

When I began to tell my story in schools, I was very anxious for Lola to tell me everything that she remembered. She had moved to Tucson Arizona, and Jean and I would visit her often. I tried to get her to tell me her story. She was reluctant to talk to me about her experiences but would often come back to the day of the deportation.

She would tell me how she held on to Frania's hand and urged her to stay with her. She repeated over and over these words, "I held on to Frania's hand, I held on to Frania's hand, I held on to Frania's hand." I think that she was trying to absolve herself of the guilt she felt at losing Frania. Frania suddenly tore herself away from Lola and went looking for their mother.

I hope that she found mother, and they gained strength from each other as they boarded the cattle car that would take them to their death. For a long time I was angry with Frania. Why did she not make the choice to save herself? I would have had a loving sister. It is only lately that I think of Frania as a courageous young woman. Her love for her mother was so great that there was no way she could abandon her. In doing what she did she has taught me what true sacrifice is.

Isaac, Dad, and I walked to our factory where we would be living, until the deportation was complete. Mr. Kapatloski welcomed his Jewish slaves to his plant. There were 20 of us, all adult males. I was the only child. The other Jewish workers did not look kindly on me; they too had little boys that were now being loaded on the death trains. When Mr. Kapatloski's son saw me, he showed his displeasure and told Isaac that I was not part of the deal. It was dangerous for him to accept an eleven year old into his factory. I was too young to get a permit, and if the Germans found out, he would be in trouble. It would be easy for Polish workers to report me to the Gestapo. Isaac answered him: "We have known each other for many years. We did business together. What do you want me do? Put him on the train and let him die?" The senior Mr. Kapatloski stepped in, looked at me, and asked me my name. I told him my name and then said, "I will be eleven in December, Sir." "You are a nice boy," said Mr. Kapatloski senior. "We will hide you in a loft, but you must obey me and your father, who is an old friend of mine. You must stay in your hiding place until all the workers leave. Do you understand me?" "Yes Sir," I answered.

I was taken to a building where I climbed a rickety ladder into a dark loft. One of Mr.Kapatloski's sons brought me some food and water and also a bucket as my toilet. The only light to come in was from the holes in the boards. I hated it. I still couldn't understand why the Nazis hated me so much. What did I ever do to them? I was praying for the men in the factory to leave so I could come down from this awful place and be with my father and brother. Finally, I heard Isaac whistling which was the signal for me to come down.

Isaac took me to a hut where the Jewish workers were staying. It felt so good to leave my hiding place and be with familiar people. All the men were talking nervously, and the only topic was about the families that were pushed into those cattle cars. A hundred people were pushed into a car that normally held 30 cattle. Before they embarked, the Polish police or the Ukrainians stripped them of all they were carrying. People heard them say, "You won't need any of this were you are going." Despite such talk, the room felt comfortable. There was a wood burning stove that made the room warm. The deportation lasted eight days. Each day the Polish workers gleefully gave the Jewish workers all the miserable details of the day.

I stayed in my hiding place, but I didn't know how long I could tolerate it. There were big rats running around that unnerved me. I was wondering to myself if staying alive was worth these indignities, but then I remembered my mother's pleading with me to keep myself alive. If I could strike back at these murderers, I would be satisfied.

One evening, after the Polish workers had left their jobs, I made myself comfortable in the backroom. The door opened and in walked two German security police. They looked my way, and I thought this is the end of the road for me, but they ignored me and asked if a known shoemaker was there. They were carrying with them a single highly polished riding boot. They asked if the shoemaker would make them such a pair of boots. He assured them that it would be his honor to make them the best boots in the world. So with that they left us, and we all gave a sigh of relief.

A day later two Polish Secret Service men walked in. Isaac's face lit up in recognition of these two who were friends of his from before the war. He knew them socially but they quickly made it clear that they didn't come here in friendship. They demanded that Isaac turn over all our valuables to them. When they had all our possessions, Isaac turned to them with tears and asked, "I thought that you were my friends?" They replied "Be glad that we are not taking you with us." I felt so sorry for Isaac--they had humiliated him so. I was so angry that I wanted to take revenge. I would fight these robbers with my bare hands. Father was crying softly for Isaac. I think that Dad was worn out. How can a father stand by and be totally defenseless?

Father was a man of action; he had fought with his brothers for Poland's independence, only to be treated badly by his fellow countrymen. He was not himself since Ronia's murder. He blamed himself for everything. He told Isaac and me to remember that his younger brother, Alex, was in America, and that if we survived, we should sell everything and go to the U.S.A. Poland was not a fit country for Jews.

After eight days, the deportation of the Jews of Piotrkow was completed. When the train reached its destination and the doors were swung open, the people saw a colorful railroad station surrounded by flowers. To the eye, it seemed like a pretty station in a small village. This scene was a German deception to give the arrivals some hope; hence they could be easily controlled.

Dudek Lefkowicz of Piotrkow gave this account of death in Treblinka. Dudek escaped from Treblinka. His story appears in *"A Tale of One City,"* edited by my friend Ben Giladi:

"They separated the women and the children from the men. The little ones were carried or walked beside their mothers, and, had no thought of the impending quick and cruel death. Their eyes were wide with fear and wonder. When they saw the stony faces of their parents, they kept silent and prepared for whatever might come. They remained stock still, nestled against one another or cuddled up to their parents, waiting for the ghastly end. Each person was given a cake of soap and told that they must bathe before going to the labor camp. The women and the children were ushered into an undressing barrack located to the left of the plaza. After undressing and placing their clothes on the ground, they were transferred to another connecting barrack. Here benches were arranged for them to sit on. About twenty men who worked as barbers entered and shaved the women's hair. It was later packed into sacks, disinfected, and eventually sent to Germany.

After being shaved, the women and children were rushed from the barrack through a beautiful 'avenue' covered with white sand into Camp II where the gas chambers were located. On their way to die they were beaten and driven by truncheons and gas pipes. Dogs were set upon them. Barking, the dogs threw themselves upon the victims. Everyone eager to escape the blows and the dogs rushed screaming into the lethal chamber. The stronger ones pushed the weaker. There was despair and agony in their screams. But the tumult did not endure long. The people tumbled down the moment they entered the chamber. Each small compartment was so filled with people that they had to lie on top of one another. Often infants and young children would simply be tossed into the rooms above the heads of the adults.

When it was no longer possible to squeeze additional people into the chambers, the doors closed with a clang. A nearby compressor extracted the air in order to save on gas. For lack of air, the people choked and their lungs exploded; thus the Nazis did not use much gas at all. The motor connected with the carbon monoxide was switched on. In twenty-five minutes at the most, all lay dead. There were no more screams. They had no room to fall down. They died standing, arms and legs entangled. Mothers and children were clasped in death's embrace, all suffocated."

Among those who were exterminated in Treblinka were my mother, sister Frania, and at least twenty close relatives.

There were hundreds of Jews like me. They hid themselves in ingenious places, staying in hiding till the "operation" was over. The Gestapo and several Jewish policemen, (These Jewish policeman were a small minority, who thought that by cooperating with the Nazis they would be saved) with the help of dogs went from house to house sniffing out the hiding places. I saw as I watched from my window, a Nazi dragging several Jews from their hiding places. The Nazi, pistol in his hand placed his gun to a man's temple and pulled the trigger. The man fell to the street, his brain scattered. The Gestapo and the Jewish policeman laughed together as they walked to the next victim.

Unlike other children who were put to death, I was fortunate not to be found. There were others like me. I later became aware of a girl Mala, who with her younger cousin Hania, was seized from her hiding place. Mala described her story in these words:

"It was certainly very frightening, and we were getting close to boarding the lorry when suddenly I left the line, went up to the SS Officer in charge, and asked him if he would allow me to go back to the Ghetto to be with my father and brother from whom I had been separated. I must have moved very fast because the guard was obviously not quick enough to shoot. The SS Officer looked at me very surprised, probably wondered how I had the courage or the audacity even to speak to him, but smiled and said "Yes".

He instructed a Policeman to take me back, and on the way I said to him, "Just a minute, I have to collect my cousin". He answered that the permission was only for me and that my cousin would not be allowed to go back with me. I found myself in an impossible situation, my heart was racing and I was terrified at the prospect of leaving Hania or loosing the chance of being reunited with my father and brother. I begged and pleaded and said that I could not possible go back and asked the lieutenant again, and I could not go back to the Ghetto without her. He eventually relented".

Not long after the great deportation, an "Action" (A Nazi order) against non-employed illegals and children took place in the remnant area of the ghetto. The Gestapo ordered all the children to be given over. I was among this group. I had not been sanctioned to live, and they were coming after me.

They rounded up hundreds of illegal Jews with my sister Lola being among them and put them in the big synagogue. There were atrocities committed in this place by the Ukrainian guards. The people were crowded without light, without food and without water. The cry of children and old people filled the air. They had to relieve themselves wherever they happen to be. Newborn babies were burned in front of the synagogue.

At the conclusion of the deportation the Nazis hung a sign at the railroad station of Piotrkow saying **"PIOTRKOW IS CLEANSED OF JEWS."** In German, the words were, "Piotrkow Ist Judenfrei." Seven hundred years of Jewish history was no more.

CHAPTER 9 | BUGAJ — SLAVE LABOR CAMP

Were we the lucky ones? My father, brother, my sister Lola, and I had survived the deportation. Lola was not with us. She had managed to avoid the deportation and had gotten a job with the Befehlstelle--a German Economic Unit that searched all of the homes of the people who had been sent to Treblinka. She and others sorted clothing and other items to be sent to Germany.

After the deportation and killings, we were assigned dwellings in the "little Ghetto"--a block of houses surrounded by barbed wire. I looked for a familiar face, a relative, or a friend but there was none to be found. I felt terribly distraught and missed my mother and sisters. We had a small room on the third floor and while Isaac and Dad went to work in Bugaj each day, I had to stay hidden. We had no idea what our future would be. The Ghetto at this point was eliminated, and the remaining Jews had to live on the premises where they worked. The surviving children became a serious concern. The Nazis felt that we were not useful as workers, rather we were "useless eaters," and we became disposable. Eventually they were persuaded to take a few children as workers. Father or Isaac must have had influence, for they were assigned to work in Bugaj which was a wood working factory. Since they were employed they were able to take me with them to live in Bugaj.

Bugaj was a slave labor camp. One thousand Jews were housed here, including about a hundred women and thirty children. We were fortunate to be assigned to this camp. The owner, Dietrich and Fisher created an enterprise that was a hoax. Their main interest in having the factory was to protect them from being sent to the Russian front. The casualties there were astronomical. It was similar to Schindler's List. I was housed with the men and we lived in one big wooden structure. Our "private" space consisted of the area around our bunks. The toilets, which were always filthy, were outside, and there was no running water. The water was carried from the well. When bed time came, I slept in my dirty clothes. Father had to coax me to stay clean. I hated cold water, especially in the winter.

They put me to work on a machine that chopped wood for the German steam operated trucks. At times I watched as plywood was being made. I watched with fascination as one layer was glued to another and a machine pressed the two sheets together. After a while the director, Dietrich, the owner of this factory, exempted kids from having to work. I spent my leisure time checking out the basement. I was intrigued with the huge boilers that produced steam to run the factory. In wintertime this was the warmest place, and the Polish man who was in charge was nice. Often he would share his breakfast of coffee and sausage. It felt good to find a Pole that was friendly and in a warm place.

I would roam the grounds and climb on the highest stack of timber. I could look over the fence and watch the outside world. I watched lovers strolling through fields, hand in hand, laughing and enjoying their youth. I was reminded with sadness of my sister Frania, who should have been able to have a similar life. I envied the birds that were free and flew over the fence. Despite the harshness, I found things to entertain me. There was a small unit of Russian deserters who joined the German army. These men were known as Cossacks. They were extremely adept at horsemanship. Even after heavy drinking, they could do acrobatics on their horses. In a gallop, they could do amazing things such as jumping off and then back on the horse. I was amazed at their antics.

The women and their children stayed in a three-story building that before the war was a textile factory. I would go there to visit Cousin Anna and her two little daughters, Rita who was eight and Ellen five. I had a real affection for the girls, and Anna. Anna was the daughter of Dad's oldest brother. She was the only female relative in the camp that I could go to for comfort. She would share with me delicacies that were not available in the camp. Circumstances allowed the entire family to remain together, and avoid deportation. Their father, Pinkus Rubenlicht, was a diamond merchant before the war, and they were once rich. It was easy to hide diamonds because they are small. Pinkus was generous and kind to me. Conditions in Bugaj were relatively good compared to other camps. But we never felt secure. Frequently, there were surprise inspections, and at such times the children hid to avoid discovery. The Nazis allowed 1700 Jews to remain. When they found out that the actual number was exceeded they sent 200 workers to another camp.

Isaac had a smuggling business. He and his friend, Helfgot, brought in food by means of the supply truck that would deliver timber. They would meet the truck and carry in sacks of potatoes and other goods. I wanted to be important and be involved. I begged Isaac to allow me to take part in his operation. He reluctantly agreed to let me come with him the next time. Isaac, Helfgot, and I met the truck, and they let me carry a sack of potatoes. I was carrying the sack on my shoulder, when a vicious dog jumped and knocked me to the ground. I was struggling while the dog was biting my behind. Along came the commandant with a hunting rifle under his arm. He called off the dog, but then he took out his revolver. He took a bullet out of the chamber, showed it to me and stated, this bullet is going to enter your head. I cried and begged him for my life. Finally, he must have decided that he wasn't going to shoot me and turned me over to the plant police.

As I entered the station I recognized the sergeant. This made me relax a bit. If I had talked the commandant out of shooting me, certainly I would be treated more kindly by an acquaintance. I pleaded with him not to hurt me, but the more I cried for mercy, the broader his sadistic smile became. I got tired of humiliating myself and cursed him. "My bottom is not made of glass." I was bent over, bottom bear, and beaten with a leather strap. The pain was great but it was worth it. It became known that I had defied this brutal man. I was a hero for the next few weeks--though I could not sit down for quite a while.

I recall another humiliating experience. The only toilets in the camp were a few holes in the ground that smelled abhorrent. I would not go there. I would find an isolated place. At one point. A Polish supervisor discovered me with my pants down. He cursed me out and made me pick up the excrement with my bare hands. I was humiliated but I could do nothing. I was a Jew, and, therefore, I was despised. It hurt more because the punishment was dealt me by a fellow Pole.

Life went on. Sundays were special since we didn't have to work. In Bugaj there were many talented people who organized entertainment to keep our spirits up. We got our news from the Polish employees that worked in the camp. We learned that the German army was defeated at Stalingrad and was retreating through Poland into Germany. Our hopes really skyrocketed later when we were told that there was an attempt on Hitler's life. Unfortunately, he was only wounded. We felt like the war was coming to an end. We were hoping that soon we would be liberated from the Nazi tyranny.

Our bubble soon burst when we heard persistent rumors that we were going to be evacuated again. This created tremendous fear in the camp. Why couldn't the Nazis leave us alone? The Germans were close to loosing the war. It was November of 1944. In a month I would be thirteen years old, normally the time, when a young Jewish boy would be Bar Mitzvah. (In the Jewish faith this is a joyous time, when one passes into manhood.) It passed unnoticed for me.

On November 25 1944, the SS guards entered the camp and ordered everyone out. I was asleep cuddling in a warm blanket. It was an awfully cold November morning. Dad got me going by bringing me something warm to drink. I was made to wear several layers of clothing. No one knew where we were headed.

The SS guards together with the Polish police lined us up, three abreast, the women and children on the left and the men on the right. We marched a short distance to the railroad terminal at the factory, and there I saw, for the first time, the death train waiting to take us away. These were the same cattle cars that brought my mother and Frania to their death in Treblinka. Was it now my turn?

I watched as Anna and her two little daughters--Rita who was nine and Ellen four were saying good-bye to their father. Anna and the children were sobbing while holding on to their father. The two girls were hugging their parents, crying and not wanting to let go.

I heard Pinkus say to his wife "As long as your eyes are open, you must take care of our girls." The Nazi SS man soon appeared with a whip in one hand and a pistol in the other, and he shouted to them to get into the car. During the commotion, while being herded with whips into the cars, I got separated from father and Isaac.

I felt terrified with the push of the crowd. I was forced into a car without my dad and brother. I was screaming to be let out so I could find my family, but the men in the car were telling me to shut up or the Nazis would kill us. I fell to the floor of this wooden boxcar and sat in a fetal position crying. This was the first time that I was alone and I felt very frightened. Crippling fear entered my body, fear that would stay with me the rest of my life.

Before this moment, I had pretended that everything that was occurring in my life was a kind of game. This was so very real. For the first time I realized the tragedy of events. There was no more going back to my fantasies. The train began to move, and during the night we felt a few cars being uncoupled. These were the cars that we knew held the women and children. What would happen to my cousins? I don't know that I cared anymore. Later I was to find out that my three cousins were sent to concentration camps in Germany. They were transported to Ravensbruck, and from there to Bergen Belsen.

They were interned with Anne Frank, author of the well known "THE DIARY OF A YOUNG GIRL." Although Anne Frank perished, miraculously my three cousins were among the survivors.

LIVING THROUGH CZESTOCHOWA CAMP

CHAPTER 10

I stopped caring. After many hours we arrived in a camp called Czestochowa in Poland. The sliding doors were jerked open and we were ordered by the guards to leave the boxcar quickly. As I left this appalling boxcar, I was hit in the face by a freezing wind. I was grateful to my father for making me wear so many clothes. I was searching for my father and brother and finally saw them. I went straight to where they were standing and hugged Isaac. They were both relieved to see me, but Isaac was bawling me out for getting separated from them.

Soon we were greeted by the Jewish head kapo of the camp. He was quick to give us a speech about the consequences of not obeying the camp's rules. I think he was very surprised to see a dozen youngsters among us. With me in Czestechowa were Lulek Lau and his big brother, Naphtali. Lulek was just seven years old and looked very puny. Lulek and Naphtali were sons of the leading rabbi in Piotrkow. We were all led to a big dark hut and found space to lie on the dirt floor. I was totally exhausted from the trip, and without anything to eat, I fell asleep. I dreamed that night of staying at my favorite Aunt Rachel's house and being tucked in bed by her under a goose feathers comforter. In the morning I was given some artificial coffee and a slice of bread. The coffee was bitter but warm; the bread satisfied my empty stomach. The kids were ordered to stay in the hut and not be seen by the Nazis.

As soon as the men went off to work, I ignored all warnings, and ventured outside to have a look. I didn't like what I saw. This was a rusty industrial plant with loud machinery and trucks everywhere. The men were filling large ammunition shells with powder, and their skin had turned yellow from working with the chemicals. The caustic nature of the chemicals causes poisoning and death. I was amazed at seeing large number of prisoners walking around with a very yellow skin tone. Although I lacked information my assumption was that these men had become very sick.

I walked to an area where tanks were being repaired. There were German soldiers working on their tanks. I stood there gazing at them as they continued to do their work. I was quite fascinated by their efforts to place a track on the wheels of a tank. One of the soldiers called me over, reached into his pocket and handed me an egg sandwich. I thanked him and ran back to the hut to eat my treasure.

Conditions in this camp were far worse than Bugaj. In Bugaj my father had access to Polish friends that would help us. Sanitary conditions in this camp were intolerable. Trips to the "toilets" made me sick. It was a hut with large planks of wood. There were holes cut into the boards. The whole interior was covered with feces. The stink was over- powering. I began to think this was as close to hell as anything could be.

After a month in this camp, I was wondering how I could survive these conditions. There were thousands of lice living in my hair and on my clothes. I tried to kill the bastards. I would gather what seemed to be a fistful of them and crush them in my hand, but there were always more. At this point my father and brother were sent to Buchenwald Concentration Camp. Therefore, if I was going to make it remaining here in Czestechowa, it would have to depend on my own cleverness and guts.

There were rumors that the Nazi commandant felt that the children were useless. He wanted the kids killed. It seems that he was personally affronted that five years after the war had started there were still Jewish children alive. This story is told by Naphtali Lau-Lavie, in his book "BALAAM'S PROPHECY." According to him, the kids were taken away and put in a special hut to be killed. However, negotiations were in progress with the Nazi Commandant to save the children's lives. The Nazi commandant was given a diamond as a bribe. Naphatali gave up his last diamond, which he had hidden in the heel of his shoe. This heroic act allowed us to continue to live.

I survived along with Lulek, and his brother. Years later, I was surprised to learn that seven year old Lulek became the chief Rabbi of Israel. His brother Naphatali Lau-Lavie, became a well known journalist and diplomat, an aide to Moshe Dayan and head of the consulate in New York.

Most of this period remains vague in my memory. I can only surmise that situations were so horrible that my memory shut down. I believe this was my defense in order to remain sane. Two months after this hell, and without my father and brother, we were once again marched to a railroad junction and packed again into boxcars. I don't have a single memory of this trip, although it lasted three days. There was no one to protect me. I would have to survive on my own guts. Could I do this? Up till now I had some protection.

I have had contact with people who have described to me the conditions of the box cars. I don't recall any of the details, massive over crowding, the lack of toilets, clean water, and the lice that continued to plague us. I was now in Germany and on my way to a concentration camp called Buchenwald.

Even though my memories are vague during this three day journey, my feelings would not fade. I recall the misery of hunger. We were all packed together to a point where movement was impossible. The inhumanity for me is wrapped up in feelings associated with the itching from the lice, the smell of human waste, and the lack of hope.

CHAPTER 11 | SURVIVING BUCHENWALD

As the train slowed, I heard noises of brakes grinding and the uncoupling of cars. The doors that were locked from the outside were opened. It was January and the air was frigid but sucking in the air felt good. I heard shouts from the SS guards to quickly empty the train. The guards were accompanied by vicious dogs that were barking and that frightened us or frightened me.

I felt despair at being parted from my family and yet I felt I had a better chance to survive on my own. I had just turned thirteen years old and had the ability to think on my feet. Even though I missed my father and brother, I could survive on my own wits and would have more freedom to maneuver. I didn't want to depend on anyone else.

We marched into the camp, surrounded by a tall electrical fence. Every few hundred yards were towers manned by soldiers with machine guns. Searchlights were constantly moving, flooding the grounds. We waited for hours in the freezing weather till we were admitted into the processing building. Since the order was that nothing could be taken inside, my bag with a sweater and blanket was discarded in a huge pile. I jumped up and down on my feet to keep warm. After a long wait I entered the building grateful to be out of the freezing weather.

My processing took me to a table. There a man in a prison uniform asked my name, birth place and age. I informed him that I thought I was thirteen but not totally certain. I was advised to make myself, at least 16 years old, in order not to be shipped out with other children. I was given number 113752. The number was written in ink on my jacket. From now on at Buchenwald, I didn't have a name, I was a number. After the early processing, we were herded into another room for disinfection. Veteran prisoners with electric shavers shaved all my body hair roughly. Next another inmate brushed my entire body with a chemical that hurt like hell. I gritted my teeth and bore it. Finally, we were escorted to a large room with numerous showerheads above us. The adults began screaming and crying out. I had no idea why they acted in such a manner, but they soon told me that they were afraid that gas would come down from the showerheads. I just stood there frozen in shock! I gladly heard one inmate say that there was no gas in Buchenwald.

Relief came when wonderful warm water descended on me. It felt so great. This was the first shower that I ever had in my life --baths had been common in Poland before the war. Next I went to a room where they dispensed uniforms. I was issued a uniform consisting of pants, a jacket, a cap and a pair of shoes. They were unable to find a uniform small enough to fit me. I was still small in stature and I was skinny. I was unconcerned about the uniform, but happy that I was rid of the lice. It was a great feeling to be clean and not itching.

We were marched to Block #52 where we became integrated with other non-Jews in the camp. The head of the block was named Wily. Each barrack was controlled by a head prisoner, a block elder. Wily was a German political prisoner who was sentenced there because he had refused to follow Hitler. He had seniority since he had been at Buchenwald for years. Wily had total control over our lives; he was in charge of distributing food and issuing work orders. He had the option of giving you an easy job in the kitchen or sending you to the quarry, where your chance of survival was poor. I sensed that he was friendly to the youngsters in his charge. At this point in the camp, survival made it necessary for each individual to look out for himself, but Willy clearly protected the youngsters from the bullies and criminals.

The bunks were wooden storage shelves, four tiers tall, which reached to the ceiling. These were very small with no bedding. We had to sleep on bare wood in a cramped position, stacked closely, with no room to turn or move. We always slept in our uniforms, and never took our shoes off for fear that they would be taken. I often felt suffocated as the larger prisoners took up a great amount of space.

Nights in the wooden bunks were especially upsetting. Many of the prisoners were very ill, and I heard many strange sounds uttered in different languages. The wetness chilled me to the bone. I often felt drips on me from above; it could have been water from the snow or urine from other prisoners – I wasn't sure. In the morning there would be men that had died during the night. We would throw the bodies to the floor, and a work group would take the bodies outside and stack them outside as if they were sacks of potatoes. It no longer bothered me to see dead people in the camp; it meant nothing to me. My feelings of compassion towards the suffering and dying had left me. I only cared about my own survival.

Morning roll call was punishing. We were aroused by shouting voices telling us to move out quickly. Our days began with roll calls where we stood for hours in the cold. Each prisoner had to be accounted for, even the dead. Sometimes I had to help drag the bodies to roll call. I felt it necessary to take anything useful from the dead bodies for myself. Shoes were a treasured item.

At one point while I stood there freezing, I looked to my left and saw a huge chimney belching out fire. This puzzled me because I had thought that chimneys let out smoke, not flames. I was told that on the chimney was written that the only way out from Buchenwald was through the chimney. I was seeing the crematorium where the dead bodies were burned. Prisoners were not gassed at Buchenwald but those who died were burned there.

There were many sadistic games that the SS officers put us through. We were often harassed by foolish commands, like attention "caps off, "caps on", singing the camp's song. After standing for hours without relief, prisoners were beaten if a yellow stain appeared on the snow. Many men who had endured harsh conditions for long periods were mere skeletons. They were called "Musselman." Their eyes were like hollow sockets. They had no control over their bodily functions. As they shuffled along, they reminded me of the walking dead. I asked myself would I soon look like them.

I had a close friend named Harry, whom I had known from my hometown of Piotrkow. Harry and I had a long history together. We had worked in the glass factory in Piotrkow and then worked together in Bugaj. My fondness for him developed from his personality. He was a very mild mannered shy boy, who didn't speak much, but I trusted him. He was considerably larger than I and very protective. He had a way of comforting me during the harsh times. We were opposites that complemented each other. We were inseparable and we spent most of our time together, staying away from the older boys. I am not proud of the fact that I often had an attitude of being above the others. I felt my family was socially more elite. By thinking that I was special, it allowed me to think that I would survive.

A few weeks after our arrival, I had a chance to explore the camp. It was enormous; it resembled a city spread over a large area. The difference was that we were prisoners, not citizens, of the camp, and there were no women or girls at Buchenwald. Beyond the fence and watch towers, there was a large forested area. The camp was split by roads and fences that separated the camp into sections; each of the sections consisting mainly of different nationalities. Among this variety were Hungarians, Poles, Russians, French, and numerous more. Some prisoners who could not endure this life threw themselves on the electrified fence, thereby ending their struggle. Some inmates, seeing their still bodies clinging to the fence, said that they envied the dead. I questioned whether I would survive, but my will to live, to avoid the fate of those on the fence, was very strong. I felt a rage against the Nazis. I would never give the Nazis the satisfaction of dying. It was almost like a cruel game to me. Each day that I woke up alive was a victory over the Nazi beasts.

Out of the need for food I would go exploring. I was told that my best bet was to beg for food in certain areas. I would stand for hours outside the compound where the Scandinavian prisoners were housed. My hope was that they would take pity on me and share their delicious parcels that they received from the Red Cross. However, I had no luck. I usually came back empty handed.

Most of the time I was hungry. In the morning we would get a 4 oz. piece of bread and ersatz (artificial) coffee. On some days, we would receive a bit of margarine. In the evening, we received hot soup that contained some potatoes and a slice of bread. Some evenings we would get nothing to drink, so I would melt snow and drink it.

One evening after our "meal," I noticed someone with a cigarette. Quickly a line formed and each man took a puff on the cigarette. For this privilege they had to pay with a slice of bread. Others who had no bread stood by another inmate, inhaling the smoke from the other's mouth. That scene made an ever-lasting impression on me. I never allowed myself to start smoking cigarettes.

As luck would have it, Harry and I were assigned to a bricklaying crew. The boss of this crew was a Dutchman and, though stern and firm, he treated us well. The work itself was not hard. Harry and I would gather the bricks, clean them, and hand them to the bricklayer. We worked to build a freezer in the central kitchen of Buchenwald. This job had its rewards; the inmates who worked in the kitchen slipped us extra food. Often we were even able to eat our meals in the kitchen; at this time we got thick soup and bread.

At the end of our working day, as we left the kitchen, we were searched by a camp policeman. For several weeks after our assignment to the brick commando working in the kitchen, we were successful in smuggling out food. Harry and I were taking awful risks. We would smuggle out potatoes and bread in the legs of our pants. We were encouraged by the kitchen workers to take more and to hand over the food to them when they were in their blocks. Our boss, the Dutchman, warned us against stealing food from the kitchen because this could result in severe punishment.

Of course, neither Harry nor I listened to the warnings and

we continued with the smuggling. This was good for the prisoners because they got additional rations, and being a young boy, I didn't think I would be caught. In all honesty, it was thrilling to break the rules. One day when we left the kitchen we were thoroughly searched and the guards found food on Harry and on me. These were inmate camp police, and what we did was a serious offense. The situation was considered serious because stealing food from the kitchen meant stealing food from everyone. Harry and I became deeply concerned because we had images of doing hard labor in the stone quarry. I pleaded with the officers to go easy on us. Loosing this job, which was light work and was inside, sheltered from the cold, was punishment in itself. Harry and I spent a day working in the quarry. The Nazis supervising work in the quarry were the most sadistic of all. Few prisoners came out alive. I have no specific memory that could confirm this.

Jack Weber who was a long-term survivor of Buchenwald wrote a memoir after the war called "Saving the Children." He told of the Jewish underground in Buchenwald, and how men in the camp underground, with the cooperation of the larger resistance movement, had decided in 1944 and even earlier to save the children. Buchenwald was a working camp. You had to be sixteen years old to get a work permit. Children were not considered useful at hard labor; therefore they were vulnerable to disposal by the Nazis. Youngsters were herded together into a special holding pen to wait for transportation to their likely death.

The orders and administration of the camp was in the hands of long time prisoners. This group of Communists and Socialists had been in prison because of their opposition to Hitler. This group of underground administrators was able to change my age from thirteen to sixteen by falsifying records and assigning me to a brick commando work group.

A decision was made by the underground that Harry and I would be moved to Block 66 in the little camp, which was a children's block. The little camp was separated from the larger camp and fenced with barbered wire with a guard at the gate. The physical area where Block 66 was located was also a holding ground for Jewish prisoners who would be sent to various slave labor camps, outlying camps in the Buchenwald system, and for many this meant death under harsh conditions.

Harry and I arrived at Block 66 and were met by Gustav who was the authority in Barrack 66. Gustav was a tall Polish Jew with reddish hair. He wore a military uniform and shiny boots. We knew who the boss was; Gustov had an air of authority. I discovered in time that he could be a decent guy. Harry and I quickly felt that we were safe in his care. At times he would entertain us with stories of Jewish heroes that fought against foreign occupation. Despite our situation, conditions in Block 66 were better. The sleeping arrangements were decent, and we were able to receive portions of the Red Cross packages that were shared with the children's bloc by other prisoners. Adults were allowed to come from other parts of the camp and meet with us. These adults provided moral support by telling us Jewish resistance stories, and giving us hope that we would survive and go on to a better life. This was substance for us as much as the food that they gathered and put into our mouths.

In the "small camp" I came into contact with many people from my hometown. I met the former president of the Piotrkow Ghetto, Szymon Warszawski. He was very happy to see me and embraced me warmly. Other boys and I were interviewed by Gustav to determine if we were ever mistreated by other Jews, who had been in positions of power in the Ghetto or in previous camps. I told him that I had no recollection of being treated badly, but recounted the story of how Mr.Warszaski had once saved my life. He intervened at one point when I had been lined up by the Nazis to be shot. I think that my words may have saved Mr. Warszawski's life, but, unfortunately, he died a few months later. The men who were found guilty of crimes against their fellow Jews would experience a strange justice in the camp. A gang of men would strangle them during the night. The Nazis never questioned these deaths, or any others, as long as the paperwork was correct. Gustav was the leader of this group that dispensed harsh justice. I think that he really enjoyed this work.

I have an indelible memory of my last meeting with my father. He came across me as I was standing with my friends in the compound. My father cried with joy when he saw me. He hugged me as tears ran down his cheeks. He had lost a lot of weight and he looked very weak and emaciated. He took a piece of bread from the knapsack from his shoulder and he handed it to me. The gesture of the bread showed his great love for me, since these were the only provisions he had for his transport out of Buchenwald. I took the bread, but I felt agitated and uncomfortable. Here standing before me was the one person in the world that I loved more than any other, and yet I was incapable of feeling affection. I bore no resemblance to the son that he knew. Sevek, the fun loving, affectionate, boyish kid was dead. I now was more like an animal, with instincts only for survival. Likely he was being sent to his death -- I am unsure under what conditions we met -- and yet I was silent. I turned my back on my own father without giving him the slightest bit of encouragement or acknowledgment.

Who was I? What kind of an animal had I become in the camps? This encounter was so powerful that it stayed with me for the rest of my life. Guilt plagued me and caused me to believe that I had betrayed my father. I left my father standing alone and walked back to my block to be with the young people. "Old people had no right to live; they were taking resources from the young," I thought to myself. My God, I was beginning to think just like the Nazis.

I had been in Buchenwald for nearly four months and conditions during that time were deteriorating. As the German began losing the war, they retreated into Germany. As the Allied armies advanced, the remaining Jewish camps were emptied and the Jews that survived were forced to move in death marches and on trains to the west, including to Buchenwald, a distribution point. Many did not survive the death marches but others did and it was at this time that Buchenwald became most congested. With this heavy influx of people, 38,000 prisoners now grew to an excess of 60,000 in the camp. The system collapsed. Discipline and order that were once the hallmark of Buchenwald disappeared. There were no uniforms for the new prisoners; the numbers ceased to be given out; even the registration process was abandoned.

Where conditions in the camp had been poor and harsh. They now became unbearable. There was severe overcrowding, increased disease and spreading malnutrition. Many of the new arrivals suffered from horrible bouts of dysentery where they had no control over their bowels. Typhus, which before was not a problem, now became rampant. Thousands of new arrivals, especially those that came from Hungary, died quickly. I was among the Polish Jews who were more numerous among the East European veterans of the concentration camps. We had been living under these conditions for five years and were much more able to adjust than the Hungarian Jews, around whose heads the Holocaust fell sharply and quickly during 1944.

CHAPTER 12
THE FINAL DAYS OF BUCHENWALD

It was now April 1945. The war was coming to an end. We knew by the thunder of artillery moving toward us that the American Army was getting very close. At one point bombs actually hit the camp from air artillery and many people were injured or killed. Again hopes ran high that the Americans might soon liberate us. But once more for me it was not to be. With Germany confronting total defeat, with the Nazi armies routed and in retreat, the Nazis still pursued their mad mission to destroy the remaining Jews.

Orders came down from the Nazi SS guards for us to present ourselves at the parade grounds. The Nazis were so fanatical that they demanded that the Lageraltester (the inmate camp leader) identify the Jews. Gustav had us rip off our yellow triangles with the letter "J" for Jew. When we were all assembled on the parade grounds, the Nazi officers called for all Jews to step forward. We were told before that we were not to obey this order so nobody from our block moved. The Nazis ordered the top leader of the prisoners give the command, but he also refused. In frustration the Nazi officers dismissed many of the prisoners, but not us. While many of the officers stood around with disinterest there was an SS officer who was especially sadistic. The young people that remained were subjected to further humiliation. He came close and ordered us to drop our pants. His intention was to examine our penises for telltale signs of circumcision. At that time in Europe only Jews circumcised their sons as part of their religious observance. He laughed gleefully at our shame.

Since we were identified as Jews, Harry and I were marched under guard into a big building. In this crowded warehouse we were among hundreds of Jews who were also rounded up. I recall the reunion with my uncle Rolnick, and his two sons, Isaac and Shlomo. We were surprised and delighted that we had been reunited and embraced each other. For a brief moment I allowed myself to feel joy. Unlike the meeting with my father I felt no responsibility. These were my favorite cousins. They were young men, only five and six years older than me. I had often stayed over night in their home, and remembered the wonderful times. We would roughhouse together, and they would carry me on their backs or give me rides on their bicycles. Their mother, Rachel, was my mother's older sister. I loved the way she gave me attention and spoiled me. I came to her when I felt that I was wronged, and she always took my side. She would give my mother an earful about how badly I was being treated. I especially liked harvest time. They had a big vegetable garden, and I would help dig up the potatoes. It fascinated me how something that I couldn't see on the surface would, when dug up, result in such abundance.

I was standing with these family members when the door opened, and the Nazi guards with submachine guns in their hands selected about fifty Jewish men and took them out of the building. We had no doubt about the fate of these fifty men when we heard machine gun fire. I walked over to where Harry was standing. His face was ashen with fear. We had come so far. To die now in this horrible, nasty place, just days before the end of the war, seemed so unfair. There had to be a way of saving ourselves.

As I gazed out the window I noticed a few prisoners had passed by the guardhouse unnoticed. The guards would just let them by. I wanted desperately to escape; I refused to die in this place, I simply would not die. Once again, I was given yet another chance to live. It came in the form of a man from the underground that I consider my angel. He spoke to me in German very softly, and he told me that Harry and I should leave the building, go outside, and find something to carry in our hands. There had been arrangements made to allow us to pass by the guards. I wasted no time in telling Harry to follow me. It is remarkable that once again we were given a reprieve from certain death.

Having escaped the crowded mass of people inside the warehouse, our next task would be the most difficult. It was important that we could make our way beyond the guards and the barbed wire that had imprisoned us. At this point it was important for us to appear as outside workers who had permission to leave the compound. We were lucky to find a container with handles on both sides. Harry grabbed one side, and I grabbed the other and with great hesitation and fear we proceeded to walk by the SS guards. One of the guards took no notice and smiled at us, but the other, an officer, shouted for us to "halt." As we dropped the can, I felt my heart pounding in my chest. We heard bullets whistling by, but with adrenaline rushing we ran like hell. This close call led me to believe that again someone was watching over me.

We slipped back to our block, thinking that we would be safe. Unfortunately we had no realization that things had changed. In contrast to before, Gustav could not and would not protect us. Instead, waving a baton in his hand, he ordered us forcefully to go to evacuation. His change of personality unnerved me. He acted now like a Nazi. I later learned that the underground in Buchenwald had made a decision to stage an uprising and the turmoil made it difficult to safely keep the children. Those who had been identified for transport would be let go. There was no hope for us. I was exhausted and very hungry and I had no energy left. I resigned myself to whatever fate lay in store. Shortly after these thoughts my spirit returned. Anger overcame me and with it the will to survive also again returned. I told myself, "I will not die. I won't give the Nazis the satisfaction. I am my dad's favorite, I am special, and I will live."

My escape on that day is made even more remarkable by the facts of what occurred to the others in the warehouse. All the remaining Jews were massacred later that same day. Among them were my treasured family members, including my uncle and cousins. The irony of this event is that it happened just a few days before the end of the war. I hated the Nazis even more for murdering my remaining family members, for killing right up to the end of the war.

CHAPTER 13

OUT OF BUCHENWALD

Despite the hopelessness of the Nazi struggle, their insanity continued. We heard that the Nazi commandant had orders to destroy the camp so evidence of their crimes would be forever erased. Imagine the spectacle that 3000 prisoners lined up, four abreast, waiting for the gates of Buchenwald to be opened. The column consisted of mainly Russian prisoners of war, who in appearance were young and healthy.

Although I had no idea where we were going, moving beyond the barbed wire and the darkness of the camp, gave me a sense of well being. For the last five years I was in one cage or another, but now my world opened up to the area beyond the fence on a warm spring day. The German countryside was flush with the colors of spring. At this point I forgot for a moment the circumstances of my departure.

In front of me walked a father and son, who I believed were Hungarian Jews. The father appeared to be forty and the son was a teenager. The father, despite his age, appeared to be emaciated and physically exhausted. A half an hour into our march the father turned to his son and told him that he could not walk any further. The son was desperately attempting to urge him on. The son took his father's arm and draped it around his shoulder and they continued to walk, but a few minutes later the father tore himself away from his son. The father covered his eyes with his hands and as he moved to the ditch on the side of the road he stopped and shouted with all his remaining strength the watchword of our faith "HERE OH ISRAEL, THE LORD OUR GOD, THE LORD IS ONE." With that, he fell into the ditch. The son was crying to his father to stand up, but the guard was there with his rifle, and all I heard was a shot as we continued to march. What I had just witnessed would stay in my memory forever. I was so moved by the love of the son for his father. I compared this to my own relationship to my father and I felt unworthy...

The column finally arrived at the Weimar railroad station. There was such contrast here for everything seemed so normal. People were walking around, nicely dressed, as if things were normal. There was no acknowledgment of our presence. Most people ignored us, some diverted their eyes. The civilian population had little sympathy for our plight. It was April 10, and we were being marched to the rail line to board a train. Buchenwald was liberated by American soldiers on April 11, and some 920 children were found there. Those of us being marched to Weimar would not be liberated until several weeks later. Some would not be liberated at all.

CHAPTER 14 | THE TRAIN TO NOWHERE

Waiting for us at the station was another train, but not a sheltered boxcar. The train had open freight cars. The young people managed to get in together in one car. We were crowded, but we preferred to cluster closely together. There was advantage in numbers. Harry and I moved to the far end of the car and leaned against the wooden sides. There was no room to sit down it was so crowded. I had on a jacket and a hat with earflaps that pulled down over my face. I was angry for being here. I felt that my family had not protected me enough, and I hated the whole world and especially God. I hated the Nazis.

All at once it started to rain and immediately I was totally soaked. There was no way we could protect ourselves from the weather. We huddled together to prevent the water from soaking us. When darkness fell, the train began to move. Now began a journey that would last for three weeks. In normal times it would have taken only five hours to arrive at our final destination.

Germany was destroyed. The railroad tracks and everything else were bombed almost constantly from the air by the American Air Force. Our train mostly traveled at night. Most of the time, we were standing in some siding. We were not fed. The two days of rationing that we got in Buchenwald was quickly devoured and gone. Hunger assailed me. I felt cramps in my stomach. I hadn't put anything in my stomach for four days. The guards, who were mostly in their fifties and sixties, stopped the train while they cooked their meal. The smell from their cooking drove me crazy.

They would let us out of the cars briefly and we could scavenge food from the fields around us. I found a few rotten potatoes and Harry found some beets. Some of the other boys were luckier--they broke into a house and found a sack of grain. Our immediate group consisted of four boys, Harry and I and two more boys all about the same age. We cooked our food over an outdoor fire, and it was the finest meal I thought I ever had. Custom dictated that we could not eat it all. All the other boys were entitled to a "sampling" of one spoon- full. I have no idea how this custom began, but this cooperation between the "boys" saved many lives especially among the weaker boys. With the cold weather and starvation, many of our boys died. In the morning we would take their bodies and carry them to the last car in the train. We would dump them among the hundreds of skeletons already collected there.

One night our train passed through a large German industrial city. We had arrived in the midst of an air raid, and the noise of the exploding bombs was deafening. It seemed like the whole place was on fire, and yet our train was snaking its way through all this destruction as if nothing was going on. In the third week of this journey, the elderly guards took us to a river so we could wash up and bring some water back to the train. Harry and I were delighted to see water. We dipped our faces in the river, and for the first time in weeks we washed thoroughly. On the way back, I left the column and knocked at a door of a house. An elderly German woman opened her door; I was begging her for food. She left for a moment and came back with a small loaf of bread. I was so happy I could have jumped for joy. My God, a whole loaf of fresh bread!

But not everyone was happy. The Russian prisoners of war protested that a Jew should not have the bread. The elderly guard supported me and let me keep my bread after cutting off a piece for his own use. I was tempted to eat the rest of the bread myself, but I controlled myself and shared it with my group.

People were dying in large numbers and the wagon in the back of us was filled to the top with corpses. Some of the Russian prisoners cut off pieces of human flesh and ate it. As much as I was starving, I could not bring myself to do that. None of our boys did. We took grass and we put it in a tin cup, added water and we warmed it. I tried to swallow it, but it would not stay down, I kept throwing it up. My determination was strong. There was the great need to feel something in my stomach.

In addition to the elderly German guards, who on the whole were not as mean as the Nazi SS guards we knew in Buchenwald, we had Ukrainian guards who were extremely sadistic in their hatred of Jews. They would shoot at us when we were searching for food. They would kill us just for fun. The German guards understood that the war was lost for Germany, but the Ukrainians had nothing to lose. If the Russians captured them they would be dead. They had deserted the Russian army and had gone over to the German side.

The agony of the trip continued. There didn't seem to be any destination in the minds of the Germans. We would start in one direction, and then we would be switched to another. Everything was in chaos as the American Army captured one German stronghold after another. American planes were constantly in the air and struck and bombed everything that moved. One day a couple of American planes made a dive for our train, but as they flew over us we started waving and shouting at the planes. The planes held their fire and flew away.

In one particular place, our train stopped for maybe five days. We were allowed to get off the train and stayed outside during this time. A small SS detachment arrived from the town, and set up their machine guns facing each other across a field. Past the railroad tracks we saw civilians walking and gazing at us in a friendly manner. We had left Germany and were now in German-occupied Czechoslovakia. These German military soldiers were chatting with each other in a cheerful way, never looking at us. To them we were just animals. I got the feeling that they would be surprised to learn that we were human at all. If you ran across their line, they would machine gun you down without the slightest regret. I kept looking at these two machine guns, and wondering, what would it feel like to have the courage to run across and into freedom? I knew that if some of the bigger boys had decided to make a run for it, I would be with them. What always surprised me was that the Russian prisoners of war could have easily overcome the few Germans guarding us, and yet they seemed to be more frightened than the rest of us.

As the train continued on its journey, more people died from starvation and disease. We had already lost half of the original group. I was again covered with lice. I lived in total filth. Human waste was everywhere, but strangely the smell didn't bother me anymore. On the days we weren't moving, all my energy was devoted to finding scraps of food.

In one large railroad junction, German military trains were standing just a few feet from us. The miserable Ukrainians were guarding us and didn't allow us off the train. Our hunger was so great that a few of us jumped off our freight car and went across to where the German soldiers were sitting in carriages eating their lunch. Each one of them opened a can of sardines. I stood with my tongue hanging out begging them for a little food. The Ukrainian guards fired at us as we were standing there begging for food. One of the kids got shot, but I did not move from this spot. The shooting of my friend had no effect on me. I was going to get some food. One of the officers looked straight at my face and reached into a basket and threw at me a large piece of ham. That piece of meat probably saved the life of Harry and me.

Finally, after more than three weeks of hell, we arrived at another camp, Theresienstadt, in Czechoslovakia. This was unlike any camp I had seen before. It was a town with paved streets and sidewalks with buildings and stores. I saw little children and old people sitting on benches reading. We were all so astonished to see such a sight. It was like arriving from the slums of Bombay, India, and finding a Four Seasons Hotel. As the train was pulling in, Czech people were standing alongside the train and some threw food and flowers at us. A picture exists of our open car with several of us standing in it, waving.

This was such a startling experience. I couldn't believe that finally there were people all around who didn't want to kill me. I welcomed the food, but of what use are flowers? Can you eat flowers?

The guards were startled too. They pointed their rifles at us, but a Czech man pulled out a gun and he told them that he would blow their heads off if they shot. They dropped their rifles and vanished. It appeared that all the German units in the camp had fled, and the day that we longed for was here. Freedom! We were liberated. No more killing, no more hunger. Who could understand what that meant?

The authorities would not allow us to leave Theresienstadt. They were afraid that we were carrying disease. I wasn't feeling well. My forehead was hot; I needed assistance to get off the train. Herman Rosenblat walked over to me and helped me to get out of the open freight car. Herman was three years older and much taller. We walked to a building where we were to be quarantined for eleven days. I was told to strip off the clothes I was wearing, and then they shaved off all my hair, the same procedure that had been done to me when I arrived in Buchenwald. But this time the barber, and everyone around me, was gentle and reassuring. He saw that I was sick and he called personnel to take me to the infirmary.

By then as I was burning up with fever. I had contracted the worst disease of the war, the dreaded typhus. Typhus causes a very high fever. Your brain literally burns up and you die, or, as happens with some, the temperature drops and you recover. It is highly contagious. They transferred me to a make-shift Russian military hospital. I was placed in a ward with many others who suffered with typhus. I was just lying there, most of the time unconscious, but every once in a while I would become conscious just to fade away again. Something was working for me. In my unconscious state, I thought I heard the voices of my family telling me not to give in. I wanted to follow these voices and be with my mother and father, but as I would get close to them, they would fade away. I woke up from this dream and everything felt so fantastic. The temperature had dropped. I was going to live! I was ravenously hungry.

The medical people seeing me regain consciousness came to my bedside smiling. My attitude had improved and I was physically much stronger, although not completely well. It was a pleasant shock to the staff that I had lived through such a serious illness. Most victims of typhus were not so lucky. I was relocated to a house to complete my recuperation. With me were others who were also recovering. I felt comfortable with the good food, clean bedding, and the caring attention I received from volunteers that had come from England to help us.

Despite all these efforts and my great improvement there was something missing. Fear set in. Was I now all alone? What would happen to me? How could I survive in the future? I had nothing, not even a dollar in my pocket. Who would take care of me? I was thinking these morbid thoughts when I heard my name, Sevek, being shouted from the street below. I ran to the window and, lo and behold, there stood my big brother, Isaac! I ran down the stairs into the street and we embraced. We were both astonished that we had survived and finally reunited. I felt that my emotions were selfish. I wanted Isaac to protect and care for me. Isaac, on the other hand was beaten down physically and emotionally. The irony was that we were delighted to be reunited but this also brought our memories back of our lost family. We had no idea who else might have survived from our family.

Isaac, who had learned that a group of children had arrived from Buchenwald, had walked the streets shouting my name. Isaac didn't look good. He was so skinny, and his eyes were sad like he had been crying a lot. Isaac looked into his knapsack and brought out a bar of chocolate. Wow! This was the first candy I had eaten in five years.

It was common for all survivors to have lengthy discussions about the whereabouts of relatives. We couldn't abandon hope that someone in our family had survived. The reality was that only a handful of the three million Polish Jews had survived the war, a couple of hundred thousand. When Isaac questioned me about our father, I explained to him that I had contact with father in Buchenwald, and that he had been shipped out to a slave labor camp in Germany. I was short in my answer because I had guilt about what I felt was my abandonment of my father. I was conflicted by my ugly thoughts that had father dead. This was not because I didn't love him. I was frightened that I would have to look after him. Even though I was free, I still found myself totally focused on my own survival and felt guilt about having survived.

We thought that Lola could have survived the war, but neither of us knew. People were traveling all over Europe trying to find any family members who had survived the war. A few weeks later Isaac had news about Lola and my Aunt Rachel. Lola had survived and was living in Germany in a displaced persons camp. We also learned from Lola that Aunt Rachel had survived Bergen Belsen concentration camp, only to be murdered by Poles in our home town of Piotrkow. Then news reached us that Father had died in February 1945 in a place called Miltelbau Boelcke-Kaserne, Germany. Dad was 55 years old when he died of hunger and exhaustion. Remarkably, his death certificate states that he died of a heart attack.

My Aunt Rachel Rolnik had returned to Poland to our hometown of Piotrkow. She, like most survivors, was desperately looking for her family. She went to her old neighborhood and entered her house, which was now occupied by Poles. She made a deal to sell her house to them. She had no desire to live in Poland. She most likely had news that her husband and her two sons were murdered five days before the end of the war in Buchenwald. I last saw them at the time of Harry and my escape. Since she was the only survivor in her immediate family, she had plans to go to Germany and stay in a displaced persons camp. My aunt received cash from the sale of her house. She was robbed and then killed in Piotrkow. She is buried in the Jewish cemetery in Piotrkow. Though I have never returned to my home town, Aunt Rachel's memory gives me the desire to return and visit her grave site.

All hopes faded when all our losses were discovered. In addition to father and Aunt Rachel, we had information that mother and my youngest sister had died in Treblinka. The realization that so many had died at the hands of Hitler overwhelmed me emotionally. I refused to accept it and my emotions turned again into rage. I now was an orphan. The dreams that a young boy has were gone. There would never be a normal life for me. All the things associated with family would never exist. The things that bind us to our family, community and the sense of being part of something were wiped out by these tragic events. I had misgivings that I would ever become whole. I wondered if I would have a future.

In my desperation I lost all my belief in my family values. I thought I would never again believe in God. I hated all the religious people who still believed in a loving God, they were such fools! "I hate you God, I screamed. Go ahead and kill me. I don't care." For hours I stomped the pavement with my feet and walked all over Theresienstadt. I was exhausted. And yet I again wanted so much to be able to cry, but tears would not come.

I didn't reach out to anyone to help me with my grief. I felt it would be a burden to the other boys for they had similar experiences. My brother was emotionally not available to me. His attitude was "Why talk about it, what good will it do?" I started internalizing the fact that the horrible details of the Holocaust are better forgotten.

I was free and being taken care of but I didn't belong to any country. I had no citizenship. Our experiences in the Holocaust and the extermination of our family made us all feel that Poland was not a fit country for Jews to live in. No matter where I ended up, I was adamant that I would never return to Poland. Most of us were hoping to live in a Jewish state of Israel. We were being prepared and trained for the difficult task of becoming pioneers in the founding of the state of Israel. We were given training in various aspects of life in a new state. A group known as Zionist would take us into the Czech countryside on marches. The countryside was beautiful, and I especially liked passing fruit orchards where I picked peaches from the trees. Our leader rebuked me for stealing food, but I didn't understand. I felt that this was a necessity of life.

Isaac told me that Lola would be coming to Theresienstadt from Germany. I don't recall that I showed much enthusiasm at this news. I still remembered as a young boy how her criticism had made me feel bad. Lola in order to reunite with us made a long and treacherous journey from Germany to Theresienstadt. When I met her, she was pleased to see me, but she offered no hugs and shed no tears. Lola, although older and thinner, looked attractive. However her eyes looked sad, and I never saw her smile. She spoke in Polish about her experiences in the war. She had been in three German concentration camps. In the last one called Nechareltz, she was beaten on the head causing her eardrum to puncture. She was staying in a displaced person camp in Landsberg, Germany. At the time of her visit it became apparent to Lola that my education had ceased six years ago. When Lola discovered that I could not tell time, she decided to teach me. Using a large alarm clock, she showed me the difference between the long hand and the short hand. It was not easy for me to catch on, and Lola became frustrated and called me stupid. That hurt. I already believed that I was not smart and to have her say that just confirmed what I already thought of myself.

While Lola was with us we heard the exciting news that we had the opportunity of going to England. The British Government gave permission for 1000 youngsters, under the age of sixteen, to come to England. We were torn about the decision we had to make between immigrating to England rather than the Jewish state. Isaac made the decision that we would go to England because he felt that our hardships were great enough, and we deserved an easier more secure life. Even though I was happy to be going to England I had misgivings. I knew nothing about this new country, and didn't know a single word of the language. Isaac was able to come with us because he was a counselor to the young people. Again it saddened us that Lola was separated from us and would not be going to England. It was her intention to return to Germany and attempt to put her life back together. During her time in a displacement camp, she had met a man she intended to marry.

The Russian Army, which liberated us, was in complete control of Theresienstadt. I was attracted to the activities of the Russian soldiers and I spent a lot of time among them. The soldiers, who were mostly young kids, were bewildered by western civilization. Few of them had ever seen indoor bathrooms or running water. They were fascinated by wrist watches and wore them as ornaments up and down their arms. The officers on the other hand were all business. They frightened me when they spoke about a forthcoming war between America and Russia. They warned us not to go to England or America and said we should come to Russia.

The Russians were raising obstacles to our plans to go to England. At first no permission was given for British planes to land in Czechoslovakia. Finally, in August of 1945 all obstacles were removed and buses took us to be transported. The plan was to allow 1000 young people to immigrate to England. However, only 732 were found and brought to Britain.

During the time of negotiations between the British and the Russian Government, we were housed in a student dormitory in Prague. I heard the staff concerns that the Russians again had made difficulties for us to depart. The boys and I were grateful for these few days of delay because it gave us a chance to tour Prague. The staff organized several groups of boys, and they took us on a tour of this very old and beautiful city. Harry and I were amazed at the size of this city, the beautiful parks and buildings, the wide avenues. I had never before been in a large city and my eyes looked in every direction so I could remember everything. More astounding was the kindness and warmth that ordinary citizens showed us. Merchants, when they found out that we were concentration camp survivors, often would give us items at no charge. My emotions thawed somewhat at their demonstrations of care and concern. It was nice to be in a place where no hatred was directed at me.

CHAPTER 15 | ARRIVING FROM ENGLAND FROM PRAGUE

Even though I was eager to leave my six years of persecution behind, I also had fear and many misgivings. Upon arriving at the airport the scenes in front of me totally amazed me. I had never seen anything similar to the RAF bombers; in fact this was my first sight of a plane on the ground. I had seen many planes including planes over Buchenwald, in the air but these unlike the small specks I had seen in the air, appeared monstrous. I didn't think that anything so large could lift itself off the ground. The crew was friendly but appeared very foreign to me. The English they spoke was unrecognizable and sounded like something I didn't think I could learn. The crew offered to share their white bread with us. Since we had never seen white bread we assumed it was cake.

I sat down on the floor in the belly of the plane with the others. There was no one among us that had experienced flying. As the plane taxied, I could sense the uneasiness that was present. I just kept my eyes shut and my hands clamped. I was telling myself not be afraid; it would soon be over one way or another. Despite my efforts to bolster my confidence I grew certain that we were going to go down each time the bomber would hit an air pocket. It was like being on the inside of a large metal tunnel, where every movement was like a sudden jolt. It was fun to watch the big boys who thought of themselves as so tough, vomiting into brown bags that the crew provided for us. I was pleased that I didn't get sick.

After many hours we landed at an English airport, which I later learned was named Crosby-on-Eden. The date was August 14th, 1945. The door of our plane opened and a small ladder came down. Isaac was shouting for me and for the youngest kids to come to the door. There was a little girl that came with us on the plane. She was no more than a year old. She was born in Theresienstadt. Three of us stood in the doorway and gently handed down this little girl to my brother who stood below me. There was a very young photographer by the name of Finkelstone who snapped our picture, and that photograph was shown in many English newspapers. I was then thirteen years old, and this is the earliest photograph of me, all others having been destroyed. I am smiling for the camera.

We got off the plane happy and yet bewildered to be on English soil. The staff of German and Yiddish speaking personnel was a bit taken back by the ages of the arrivals. They had anticipated youth between the ages of ten to fourteen. A large part of the boys were between sixteen to nineteen years old. Permission to come to England was restricted to those of us who were less than sixteen years old. However, my brother and the other counselors had simply changed the ages. I thought that this situation would be to my benefit. I will get more attention than the others because I was younger.

We were detained by the formalities that were necessary parts of coming to a new country. Immigration papers had to be filled out, but my brother handled that. After our exhausting trip we boarded coaches at nightfall, and were taken to a community area in Windermere. We were escorted to a large lit hall with many tables set up with food and drinks. Hungrily I eyed the food we all made a dash to make sure we would get our share. We still didn't trust the fact that food would be available. The staff urged us to eat slowly but no one paid attention.

After having our fill a counselor, took me and some of the smaller boys away and showed us to our rooms. I entered a small room that had a single bed and a dresser. I was delighted that I had a room all to myself. I was accustomed to living with large groups, and without amenities such as mattress and linen. I was even thinking that it was silly to have linens when straw would be fine.

The strangest thing of all was having pajamas and slippers. I was puzzled with what to do with these. I knew right away that I would have a problem with this. I would not take my clothes off. I liked to sleep with them on. Imagine how unprepared I would be if an emergency occurred. I still hung on to the idea that I must be ready if bombs were to fall, or I was expected to get up in the middle of the night when called for roll call. As I saw the other boys wearing pajamas I gave in and accepted the idea. That night I slept well. My dreams of being chased and beaten had left me for a while. As I awoke I was excited and anticipated what the upcoming day would be like.

We lined up to get our new clothes, and I was pleased with the new shirt, pants and shoes that I was handed. Some of the older boys were disgruntled by what they were given. Even though it was after the war, it was still necessary for the English to ration cloths. Since we had come out of such hardship we had unrealistic expectations of our new life. There was a shortage of large sizes so the boys had a limited choice. It was fun to watch what was going on. I just had to make sure that I received a little more than the others which would satisfy me.

I spent days being examined by medical people. My teeth were in bad shape and needed attention. I had not seen a dentist for six years, and during that time I didn't brush my teeth. I had an enlarged heart but I had no idea what that meant. It was not a concern for me at this point.

During my stay here there was one especially vivid moment. We reviewed a movie about Palestine and the Israel flag was shown across the street. With out prompting the whole group stood up and cheered. We had spent years being victims, but the flag gave us back our sense of belonging to something.

Windermere is situated in the Lake District of England and some call it a little Switzerland. Though it is very beautiful, I had little appreciation for nature. We were taken on hikes and climbed hills. At first I didn't see why I should exert myself, but after a while I liked it and was eager to hike. There were bicycles available but I had never ridden one. At the age of thirteen I had my first experience trying to learn to ride. At first it was difficult because like any novice I had some spills, but after mastering it, I found a sense of exhilaration and freedom. To this day I am an avid bike rider and have never lost that feeling.

There were so many things to experience. I was accompanied by a counselor and many of the small boys to the town of Crosby- on- Eden. I had not been in an automobile since long before the war, and it reminded me of Dad coming to pick me up in a car from vacation. I was completely amazed at what I saw. The traffic lights drew my attention. The changing of colors from red to green and yellow fascinated me. I had no clue to what all this meant, but I could see that the people were paying attention and proceeding orderly. I stood in front of store windows, frozen to the spot. How could they show beautiful looking clothes and even food protected by just a thin layer of glass? Wouldn't people simply break the glass? We stopped at a Café for tea and cakes and were served by a young lady. I tried to be on my best behavior and not take more than three pieces.

Three months passed quickly and the camp was being dissolved. Isaac had left two months ago to go to London and find work and lodgings for himself. Many of the older boys were to do the same. I was to go first to a hostel in Bedford, and from there to a hostel in Ascot to learn more English. Then the Jewish Committee for Children would decide the next step. I enjoyed staying in Windermere. I loved the care and the treatment. I left Windermere with a feeling that it was all right to trust grown-ups. This was a large change in my outlook.

Both hostels were situated in large beautiful English houses that could house up to twenty five people. Harry and I and many others had been in Buchenwald. Most of us had survived by breaking the rules and sometimes this caused chaos. I think that most of us had developed an attitude that we were entitled to be treated special since we had suffered so much. Our counselor would speak softly and try to reason with us, which took a great deal of patience. I myself thought that his softness towards us was a sign of weakness. We were still operating under the misconception that kindness meant weakness.

In the morning I would attended English classes. By now I could speak and write some English. During my leisure time I spent time playing table tennis. Harry and I played for hours at a time. Harry became a good player and at times competed against some of the English students. While in Ascot we were located near the famous race track. We had a great deal of fun on racing day. There were thousands of cars and parking was at a premium. I instinctively knew that I could profit from the situation. Without permission, I would wave cars into the yard and collect ten shilling which seemed like a fortune to me.

Clearly this was the time that I was turning into a young man, and enjoyed being in the company of young women. We met some English girls who were attracted by our foreign speech and mannerism. I closely watched how the older boys talked and interacted with the young women. I was shy and totally ignorant of proper behavior with the opposite sex. Despite my lack of education and lack of mastery of the English language, a school girl my age was attracted to me. I felt so good that she would choose me over others. Although short lived it was an important moment in my young adolescence.

CHAPTER 16
MY SCHOOL DAYS IN ENGLAND

The transition period was over. Our nutrition and medical status had greatly improved and we had had some time to get used to our new country.

Decisions were made by the Jewish Committee as to our future. Among our group some were sent to start employment, others like Harry were enrolled in trade schools. I felt fortunate to be selected to enter an academic setting where I would get an opportunity to further my education. I had regrets of leaving most of my friends behind, and especially Harry. Harry and I had been together throughout the whole war. We had known each other since the Ghetto in Piotrkow and had escaped death many times. There were times on the train that I knew I would not have lived if it wasn't for the two of us sticking together and sharing everything. We were not only friends but shared a common bond that could only be understood by those who survived the hell of the camps.

I felt proud that I was chosen to go to school. I traveled to my first school in England, called Bunce Court. I felt adventuresome to have been trusted to travel on my own, and not to be accompanied by an adult. I spoke enough English to follow directions and ask for help if I needed it. I took a bus from London to Otterden, Kent. The bus let me off on the highway that was four miles from the school. I was carrying my little suitcase with me that contained a few articles of clothing, but it held no remnants from my past life. The walk was uphill, but I didn't mind it as it gave me a chance to look at the English countryside. The scene before me was green rolling hills with scattered farms. The sheep and vivid green landscape were great contrasts to what I had previously experienced. I was seeing a prosperous countryside instead of the impoverished peasants I remember from Poland.

I was greeted by the head mistress of the school Miss Anna Essinger. Miss Essinger was a famous educator who founded a progressive Gymnasium in Ulm, Germany. Miss Essinger left Germany after the Nazis took over and came to England in 1933 with her staff and students. On her arrival in England she established a similar school which was highly reputed. She was fondly called Miss Anna by everyone. She was in her sixties when I arrived there in 1946. Miss Anna had devoted her entire life to the education of young people. She had given up at considerable cost her country and her personal life, to make this progressive school successful. I recall my first meeting with her. She was small in stature but large in her love for her students. Momentarily, because of her warmth many of my fears and much trepidation subsided. I was keenly aware of the fact that I was among very bright educated students. How was I going to compete in this environment? I felt ignorant; I didn't even know my alphabet!

Sam Oliner, one of the students who was from Poland, was assigned as my mentor. We spoke Polish and that made me feel at home. Sam took me on a tour and then to our dorm. The counselor had cubicles that were just large enough to hold a twin bed, a small dresser, and chair. As more boys joined us Sam introduced them. All of these fellow students were survivors of the camps. Willie and Leopold Flischman, were brothers from Hungary. I also met Abe Herman and Erwin Buncel. I quickly felt at ease with this group and later we developed good friendships.

The next day I was taken to a large house, known as the "Manor". It was a spacious three- story house that held a great deal of the social events. There was a large dinning room that also served as a recreation center. I sat at the table and waited for breakfast. They brought in a pot of something I had not seen before. I took some and put it on my plate, but it looked disgusting to me. The taste and texture was unfamiliar to me and I didn't like it. I skipped the porridge and satisfied myself with just toast.   At lunch and dinner they served green vegetables. I refused this also because it reminded me of grass.

I had problems with table manners. I was not used to eating with a spoon and knife especially the English way of holding the fork. The others starred at me when I quickly finished my meal. Miss Anna had me sit next to her to curb my poor table manners. She made sure that I slowed down and learn to eat properly. Anna also assigned a young female student by the name of Helen to further develop my skills.

I was to find classroom life difficult. My teacher was named Helga. Although she smiled at me and tried to reassure me, I was pretty certain that I didn't belong there. I was not in the habit of asking anyone for help, but she was so charming and sincere that I felt relieved. Despite all my struggle I enjoyed listening to the students read and talk. Despite my reluctance and insecurity, I started to pick up English and enjoy learning.

I continued to struggle academically and socially but I became good in a few subjects like Old Testament, and literature. English grammar and math totally overwhelmed me. You can imagine what it was like to skip from second grade to high school level. I had no foundation. I was still determined and Helen continued to tutor me. I was reluctant to accept help especially from a girl, but she was very patient. Very slowly I began to accept an important life lesson. There is no disgrace in asking to help.

Helen and I went for walks in the fields and explored the countryside. She would stop, and say, "Don't you just love nature?" Her question was totally lost upon me, for I still had the belief that if you couldn't eat it or possess it, it was totally useless. The other boys teased me that Helen was my girlfriend since we spent so much time together. The nicer Helen was to me the meaner I was to her. I couldn't understand how she could like me. She was nice and caring and was truly interested in me. Helen was interested about my experiences in the war and would often question me about them. I found it difficult to speak about that part of my life. Even among the survivors the past was never mentioned. I knew little about the other boy's experiences in the holocaust. I would hear Sam's story fifty years later when he spoke before an audience of students.

Although we never spoke of our living through the Holocaust, I continued to feel rage at any mention of Hitler's Germany. When a new student arrived in our dorm he spoke of the glory of the Nazis and Hitler. This seemed impossible to me because he was Jewish and also lost his family. Everyone argued with him but he could not be persuaded in his belief. I could not continue to listen to his Nazi propaganda and my anger got the better of me. I hit him with my fists and gave him a bloody nose. Sam separated us before I could beat him up some more. I thought that I was justified but Sam and the others disagreed. This attitude surprised me. Maybe they were not as angry as I was. That incident more than anything else, made me recognize that such behavior was not acceptable. I had to learn proper behavior or I would lose my friends. I continued to have a difficult time getting along with the English boys. I didn't know how to fit in. Sam was always there, letting me know in a gentle way how I needed to change. I was starting to realize that my survival conduct that served me well in the concentration camps was getting me into trouble. Changing my thinking was very difficult, but I so much wanted to be accepted.

As time passed, I began to love Bunce Court. I had no other home, and I began to feel a sense of belonging. I took part in school discussions; I asked questions in the classroom; and even enjoyed learning. I loved my teachers and became close to some of them. One female teacher, Hago, invited me to her house for tea. I thought this was wonderful. We had a music teacher that encouraged me to learn to play the piano. I practiced daily and learned to read music. Every Friday night the whole school would assemble in the dining room. There was always a music recital, a lecture, and a poetry reading. Music was the soul of this school. The faculty and the students participated in the recitals. In my second year, I played a short piece by Mozart. Miss Anna was taken aback by my appreciation of classic music, and I could see tears in her eyes. The savage part of Sevek was slowly becoming civilized. I also developed athletic skills and became the goal keeper for our soccer team.

Parents' day at school was especially difficult to deal with. When parents and family gathered at school to see their children, I was reminded of my own family. I found it hard to watch the closeness and love that others were enjoying. It was at times like this that I would retreat into my own world and become depressed. I could imagine my large family embracing me with love, had members survived. Summer vacations which most students looked forward to were not a fun filled time. My brother Isaac was engaged to be married and it was my hope that I would be part of his family. When they got married and had a child, I was no longer part of this family either.

The first summer Miss Anna had arranged for me to go with a fellow student, Albert, to his home in London. This was a very nice family and treated me well, but I felt uncomfortable. I felt that they just took me in out of pity and I hated that. I went off on my own as much as I could. The Refugee Committee had given me some pocket money so I would go to the West End of London and see two movies in one day. I liked being in London. I enjoyed the energy of the place. It was such a wonder for me to walk the streets of London and look at all the theater marquees.

I was glad when summer was over and could return to school. I was capable of developing close friendships. In addition to Sam, I became close to Irwin Buncel. He was a Czech Jew and had been in the camps. Irwin was a soft-spoken person, reserved but friendly. He hardly ever would raise his voice or get emotional about anything. He was an excellent student and good athlete, especially at soccer. We talked a lot about our hopes for the future. I was also close to Abe Herman. Abe was my age and also came from Czechoslovakia. He was good-looking and very bright. He loved the arts and played the piano beautifully. Abe was introverted and it was difficult to get to know him. He had a great smile, and I was drawn to him because, I was still struggling with my academic work. I could not get the concept of math and science. Though I now spoke fluent English and read well, learning grammar was beyond me. I felt frustrated that my friends were good students. The school did awake in me a curiosity for learning. I remembered during art lessons, I had envy toward the girls who could draw so well.

I became an avid reader to make up for lost time. My favorite author was an American, William Saroyan. I loved his books and read all that were available. I loved theatre and watched all the school performances.

I initiated the idea of holding a school dance. It was difficult to convince Miss. Anna, but she reluctantly agreed. The girls were enthusiastic and willing to join in. We gaily decorated the hall, and it was my job to find the dance music. The faculty came through with gramophone records from their own collections. This was the first dance I had ever attended. I had learned how to dance and enjoyed it. I became acquainted with a girl named Martha. She was friendly and I enjoyed dancing with her. I knew that she liked me, but I felt undeserving of her attentions. Even though I had organized the dance, and my social skills were developing, I had a long way to go.

One day while exploring the countryside on my bike I came across a cherry orchard. I was extremely fond of this fruit, especially the black bing cherries. I was ready to help myself when a man appeared and asked me if I would like to earn some money picking cherries. The idea of making some money excited me. The man pointed to a narrow ladder that was resting on a branch and gave me a basket for the cherries. It was difficult to climb the narrow ladder that rested on slim branch. I didn't feel secure, but I was determined. I managed to pick fifty pounds of cherries and earned the enormous amount of ten shillings. This would be comparable to $5 dollars. When I returned to school and told them of my adventure, some of the braver students wanted to join me. Miss Anna disapproved of the risk taking, but I was accustomed to it and continued.

A wonderful surprise came in the form of a package from Canada. When I got the parcel I took it to my cubicle in the dorm and secretly opened it. It contained treasures like chocolates, biscuits, and canned goods that were hard to get in postwar England. I called over all the boys in the dorm and shared the goodies with them. The gift came from a lady in Montreal Canada. Enclosed was a letter. Her name was Esther Gold. She wrote that she read about me in a Jewish journal and wanted to get to know me. She described her husband and two sons and her life in Montreal. It amazed that someone unknown from a distant place would care about me enough to do such acts of kindness. I continued to keep her informed and she continued for many years to be supportive and encouraging.

When I was in my second year at Bunce Court, there was debate by the staff whether I should sit for the matriculation exams. These exams given by the University of Cambridge were designed to separate the students that would be going to the universities from those that would go into trades. To pass the exam one had to pass six subjects, including English and math. Everyone in Bunce was being tutored to sit for these exams so they decided that it would be a good experience for me to sit for the exams too. Before the exam everyone studied day and night, including me. When the big day came, I was extremely nervous. We all sat at our desks waiting for the exact hour when the envelope would be open and the tests passed out. All answers had to be written. There was no such thing as multiple choices. As I read the questions, I became panic stricken. I was telling myself to relax; this was going to take five hours. I had to pass all six subjects or else fail. I thought that I had done well in some subjects, but not in English grammar. When the results were announced my predictions were true. The staff was delighted at my achievements. They were amazed that in a short time I had advanced so far scholastically. The favorable comments by my teachers could not take away my disappointment.

When I returned to Bunce Court, from my summer vacation, I was devastated by the news that the school, due to financial difficulties, was to close. I felt that again I was loosing my home. It was a cruel blow to have to give up the one thing that had restored my soul. This school had become a substitute for my family and had turned me back to a human being. I feel that this was where my journey of healing began.

CHAPTER 17 | FINISHING MY EDUCATION

The Committee made arrangement for me and Irwin to travel to London to apply for entrance to a prestigious school called William Ellis. I sat for the entrance exams and was admitted. This was a large and proper English school. The students wore school uniforms, a jacket with the school colors and a cap. The teachers, all male, wore black gowns. We all stood at attention when a master would enter our class room. When riding the subway or bus I felt proud to be wearing my new school uniform.

The school was well known and people recognized the blue and gold uniform. One's behavior in public reflected upon the school--so I was always conscious of this. If the occasion would arise I would give up my seat to an adult. After attending this school for one year, I was able to finish my studies, but I never again felt the bond I had at Bunce Court.

Irwin and I became very ecstatic when the school announced that there was going to be a trip to France. We eagerly read the bulletin board that had all the information about the trip. Irwin was doubtful that the Jewish Committee would pay our way. There were further obstacles since neither of us possessed English citizenship. We needed permission from the British Home Office to leave the country. Also authorization would be needed to be allowed back in. Irwin was ready to give up on the trip, but I was persistent. We found that we would be allowed to go if we received the proper documents. This required much red tape from the various agencies. We ran from one Government Agency to another, and with a lot of pleading we procured all the necessary papers.

Irwin and I stood on the deck of the ship, and watched the cliffs of Dover recede from our view. This was my first trip on a ship, and I was in a constant state of wonder, taking in all the new experiences. Upon our arrival in France we boarded a train to Paris. The scene outside the window was the French countryside. I paid great attention when the train pulled into the French railroad station. I was caught up in the labyrinth of crossing train track.

We were housed in a dorm with many of the other students. I told our counselor that I had family in Paris and asked for permission to spend my time separate from the group. I got the ok but had to return each night.

One of the purposes of my trip was to make contact with some relatives I had not known before. They were expecting me since Isaac had written to them. Getting in touch with them was quite a task, since only one spoke English. My cousin Rachel who was a student at the university in France was able to give me directions in English. I had quite an adventure traveling since I didn't speak French. After several hours of travel, I finally found my cousins residence.

My cousin welcomed me warmly in Yiddish. This I could easily understand and I felt more comfortable. He was a man in his sixties, a small powerfully built man, who had worked with his hands all his life. He had escaped Poland before the war. I knew very little about my cousin's past. We spoke about the family in England and my studies. His daughter Leoh, and her two girls, Rachel, and Leah, joined us.

Leoh was a widow who lost her husband in the war. I was pleased to meet Rachel, who spoke fluent English. Rachel was slender with a dark complexion and had curly hair. She had a lovely but somewhat sad smile. She was two years older than me, and attended Paris University. It was agreed that Rachel was going to be my guide and would show me the sights of Paris.

Rachel picked me up at my dorm the next morning, and I was proud to show her off to others. I had a wonderful time with Rachel. We took public transportation and visited the Louvre and many beautiful parks. Rachel was fun be with. We bought sandwiches and sat down on the grass. We engaged in conversation while looking at each other's eyes. I had acquired strong feelings for Rachel but could not express them.

On the last day of our Paris vacation, Irwin and I decided that we would spend the last evening together. We took the Metro to the entertainment district of Paris. We had very little money and couldn't afford to enter nightclubs. As compensation we bought two large bottles of wine. We sat in an outside Café and ordered two lemonades. We drank the lemonade quickly and brought out the wine, which we carried in our trench coats. We poured the wine into the glasses and began to drink. This was the first time either of us had any experience with alcohol. We had a good time drinking the wine and quickly felt giddy. I felt very at ease and liked the effect. We were determined to finish both bottles. We may have looked silly to others, but we found each other very entertaining. We were feeling so powerful that we didn't want the evening to end. Our curfew was at midnight but that had long passed. We were a little intoxicated and in no hurry to return. There was a long wait for the train but we were unconcerned because this was our last night in Paris. We boarded the ship to England, and Irwin and I stood on the upper deck feeling horribly sick.

I continued to stay in touch with my friends from Bunce Court. Abe, and Sam and Erwin lived fairly close and I frequently bicycled to their homes. They lived, like me, as boarders in people's homes. Erwin was at London University studying physics. Abe was studying architecture. Sam had a job and was waiting to get a visa to come to America. I was an apprentice in an accounting firm that specialized in theater. I took advantage of receiving free tickets, because this made me popular with the young ladies.

Soon after coming to England, Isaac contacted our uncle in Chicago. He escaped Poland in 1912 on the heels of being wanted by the police. He was wanted for smuggling arms to the Polish underground. My uncle and Aunt wrote to me, and they offered to sponsor my coming to America. I would take time to obtain all the papers that were needed. Sam had left for the USA, and I wanted to join him. My sister Lola and her husband and son were in America too. News had it that America was a big melting pot where all people could fit in. In England I stood out as a foreigner. I felt that I could make a better life for myself. I waited patiently for a letter from the American Embassy.

After long anticipation, a letter from the American Embassy arrived. I was so hopeful. Clutching the letter in my hand; I entered the Embassy. Seeing the majesty of the building and then gazing at the American flag, proudly displayed, that here I would be free and make a home. I nervously found the immigration department and was told to take a seat and wait. I was looking at the many people who were milling around, all hoping to get a precious visa, and begin a new life in America. After several hours my name was called and I found myself standing before a councilor who was sitting behind a desk reading my file. He asked me to sit down while continuing to read. A few questions were asked about my origin, and then I was asked if I was ever a member of the Communist party. I knew that I was against communism, and the only membership I ever held was that of a concentration camp survivor. And at this moment I would have been willing to set fire to the Soviet Embassy to prove it. I was asked to raise my hand and swear that everything I said was true. He told me that I would have my visa in two weeks. I left there jumping with joy. I couldn't refrain myself from shouting that I was going to America.

I was overjoyed when Gertie gave birth to her son Lionel so I felt sad when the time came for me to leave England. I was leaving behind my brother Isaac and my sister-in-law Gertie. It was especially difficult to part from my little nephew Lionel of whom I was extremely fond. Lionel's birth was terribly exciting to me. He was the first born after our liberation. He was named after my father and we considered this a victory over Hitler. Despite all his efforts to destroy us, a new generation lived on.

It was possible that this was the last time I would see Isaac, Gertie and Lionel. My friend Abe was to stay in England, but Irwin was to soon make his way to Canada.

My departure from my brother was very emotional. When it was time to take the train for my ship "LIBERTE" Isaac embraced me, tears ran down from his eyes as he was hugging and kissing my face. I had never before felt such love from my brother. I thought to myself, what a shame that so many years had passed since he was able to show this type of love. It was difficult but also reassuring that I would do well.

The train arrived at the port city of Plymouth from there the passengers were ferried to our ship SS Liberte. In the darkness the ship appeared enormous to me. It was if it was a city on water. My ticket was in the tourist class, and I was among many young Americans returning home. They were a cheerful generous group that made me feel accepted. I would join them at the tables and they seemed very fun loving. They made obvious attempts to include me. While I was sitting with them they were curious and I shared small pieces of my life while a youngster in Poland. When a young lady named Beth, heard my story of being prevented from ice skating in Poland, she replied, "I live in New York and I will make a point to take you to your first skating experience." Their attitude made me feel that in America I would be accepted as an American and not as a foreigner. Their manner gave me confidence that in America I could succeed.

On the sixth day of our trip everyone was up early and stood on the deck of the ship. I had my first glimpse of the statue of Liberty and felt welcomed. Beth kept her promise and the next day she picked me up in her own car and we went ice skating at Rockefeller Center. This is America! On the first day of my new life, I was skating, a pretty American girl by my side. I felt such a wonderful sense of freedom. Here in America everything was possible!

EPILOGUE

In 6th grade my grandfather came and told his story to my class. I looked around at my classmates, legs crossed on the gray carpet of the multipurpose room, fixated on my grandpa Sid. This was not the multipurpose room that held class Halloween parties, or the bowling unit for gym class. The room transformed as our worlds transformed. As he spoke, he connected with every 12 year old boy and girl we entered the world of Sevek. At the end, he asked for questions.

"Do you hate the Germans?" one of my friends asked.
"No," replied my grandfather.

My grandfather had done more than overcome oppression. From the ashes of hatred rose hope. He said he did not hate, and with his message, my classmates and I understood the potential of humans. We each have the ability to heal our wounds and prevent further affliction of others. My grandpa Sid has not only worked toward the healing of his own wounds, a lifetime of healing in itself, but he has worked to heal the wounds that prevent us from uniting not as Polish, or Americans, or Germans, but as people.

The world is a safe place when I'm with my grandpa. I am encouraged to express my feelings, my emotions and my thoughts feel so at ease. My haven lies within his hugs.

Rebecca Finkel (grand daughter)

Courage. Was it courage that allowed Sevek to survive the Holocaust? Some would say (my father among them) that courage is often mistaken for getting to the point of "no longer giving a damn". Sevek was presented two choices: pursue survival with a single-minded determination to the exclusion of all other considerations; or die. Courage? Sure, Sevek had to have some of that too. But unlike Sevek the child, my father Sidney had many choices. For most of his adult life, he chose to bury his past. Courageous? No. Necessary to continue surviving? Perhaps. Motivated by fear? No doubt. The way to conquer one's fear? Confront it. While my father was subjected to and witnessed the atrocities of the Nazi's, I have been witness to true courage. The courage to confront one's fears, to heal, to become whole, and to share of one's self with others.

The courage to confront one's past and conquer it; the anxiety of our first 24 hours in Washington DC awaiting our visit to the United States Holocaust Museum. My father's tension was palpable. What courage it took to make the decision to go, to get on the plane, to step foot in the museum. For the rest of us, we were walking into a museum. For my father, he was walking into his past, a dark past filled with hatred, death and fear. A past he had tried to forget, but could not, creating a void in his life that would not allow him to experience true fulfillment and peace. Stepping into the museum's cattle car, the scene of his greatest horrors, walking through, making it to the other side, breathing, returning to normal, talking about it. Actually talking about it. After a lifetime of knowing nothing about my father's past except that he was a "holocaust survivor", he was actually talking about it.

Courage. The ability to confront your fears, to allow them to come streaming through your veins. To allow your mind to remember the worst no matter what the outcome. That's courage. But that wasn't enough for my dad. Every time he speaks or writes, I know he confronts the same demons - - the fears and anxieties which come from being engulfed by evil. But for Sevek, the healing process continues. Sevek the child now has choices. For Sevek, it is no longer mere survival. For Sevek, it is true acts of courage which allow Sidney, my father, to tell his story so that we too can confront our inner-most fears; so that we too can take the courageous journey of healing.

Leon Finkel (son)